Praise for *Online Recruiting and Selection:*

"Reynolds and Weiner bring extensive experience to their extremely useful treatment of this complex topic, bringing together diverse bodies of knowledge in information technology, human resource strategy, and psychological testing and assessment."

Paul R. Sackett, University of Minnesota

"No executive or HR professional should conduct online screening or testing of job applicants without reading this excellent book. The authors not only discuss significant efficiencies that can accrue from online assessment, but also examine support systems that will ensure quality data are collected to facilitate personnel decision making."

Neal Schmitt, Michigan State University

"*Online Recruiting and Selection* is essential reading for any manager or executive who needs to make good business decisions about people in an era of ever-changing new technology."

Dr. Wendy S. Becker, Editor, The Industrial-Organizational Psychologist, *Associate Professor of Management, Shippensburg University*

Talent Management Essentials

Series Editor: Steven G. Rogelberg, Ph.D
Professor and Director Organizational Science, University of North Carolina – Charlotte

Special Features

Each volume contains a host of actual case studies, sample materials, tips, and cautionary notes. Issues pertaining to globalization, technology, and key executive points are highlighted throughout.

Titles in the Talent Management Essentials series:

Performance Management: A New Approach for Driving Business Results
Elaine D. Pulakos

Designing and Implementing Global Selection Systems
Ann Marie Ryan and Nancy Tippins

Designing Workplace Mentoring Programs: An Evidence-based Approach
Tammy D. Allen, Lisa M. Finkelstein, and Mark L. Poteet

Career Paths: Charting Courses to Success for Organizations and Their Employees
Gary W. Carter, Kevin W. Cook, and David W. Dorsey

Mistreatment in the Workplace: Prevention and Resolution for Managers and Organizations
Julie B. Olson-Buchanan and Wendy R. Boswell

Developing Women Leaders: A Guide for Men and Women in Organizations
Anna Marie Valerio

Employee Engagement: Tools for Analysis, Practice, and Competitive Advantage
William H. Macey, Benjamin Schneider, Karen M. Barbera, and Scott A. Young

Online Recruiting and Selection: Innovations in Talent Acquisition
Douglas H. Reynolds and John A. Weiner

Senior Executive Assessment: A Key to Responsible Corporate Governance
Dean Stamoulis

Real-Time Leadership Development
Paul R. Yost and Mary Mannion Plunkett

Online Recruiting and Selection

Innovations in Talent Acquisition

Douglas H. Reynolds and
John A. Weiner

A John Wiley & Sons, Ltd., Publication

This edition first published 2009

Blackwell Publishing was acquired by John Wiley & Sons in February 2007. Blackwell's publishing program has been merged with Wiley's global Scientific, Technical, and Medical business to form Wiley-Blackwell.

Registered Office
John Wiley & Sons Ltd, The Atrium, Southern Gate, Chichester, West Sussex, PO19 8SQ, United Kingdom

Editorial Offices
350 Main Street, Malden, MA 02148-5020, USA
9600 Garsington Road, Oxford, OX4 2DQ, UK
The Atrium, Southern Gate, Chichester, West Sussex, PO19 8SQ, UK

For details of our global editorial offices, for customer services, and for information about how to apply for permission to reuse the copyright material in this book please see our website at www.wiley.com/wiley-blackwell.

Library of Congress Cataloging-in-Publication Data

Reynolds, Douglas H.
Online recruiting and selection : innovations in talent acquisition / Douglas H. Reynolds and John A. Weiner.
p. cm. – (Talent management essentials)
Includes bibliographical references and index.
ISBN 978-1-4051-8230-0 (hardcover : alk. paper) – ISBN 978-1-4051-8229-4 (pbk. : alk. paper)
1. Employee selection. 2. Technological innovations. I. Weiner, John A. II. Title.
HF5549.5.S38R39 2009
658.3'1102854678–dc22

2008052111

A catalogue record for this book is available from the British Library.

Set in 10.5 on 12.5 Minion by SNP Best-set Typesetter Ltd., Hong Kong
Printed and bound in Singapore by Ho Printing Singapore Pte Ltd

1 2009

Contents

Series Editor's Preface xi
About the Authors xii
Preface xiii

Part I The Context for Online Talent Acquisition **1**

Chapter 1 The Context and Business Case for Technology-Based Recruitment and Selection **3**

Driving Factors: A Brief History of HR Technology Tools 4
The Labor Market Context: "We Need Good People!" 5
The Business Landscape: Shape Up or Ship Out 7
Growth of the Internet 9
Science-Based Selection Methods 12
The Human Resources Challenge: Better, Faster, Cheaper . . . and More Strategic 13
Efficiency and Speed 13
Insight and Predictive Accuracy 14
Strategic Impact 15

Chapter 2 The Technology Landscape **19**

Mainframes, PCs, and Client–Server Computer Architecture 20
The Internet Changes Everything 21
The Pressure to Integrate 22

New Integration Facilitators 24
The Next New Paradigm 25
Software Delivery Models in Transition 27
Behind the Firewall 27
Application Service Provider (ASP) 28
Software as a Service (SaaS) 28
Technology Trends and Software Users and Buyers 28
Customization versus Configuration 29
Software Maintenance 29
Further Reading 31

Chapter 3 Foundations for Online Assessment 33

The Role of Professionally Developed Assessments 33
Effective Selection of People into Organizations: Value and Risk 35
Purpose of Assessment 35
The Value of Assessment – Organizations Have Much to Gain (or Lose) 36
Assessment Risks 37
Essential Measurement Concepts 38
Validity 38
Reliability 42
Types of Measurement Error 43
Measuring Reliability 44
Score Interpretation 45
Professional Practice Standards and Legal Considerations 48
Professional Standards and Principles 48
Fair Employment Laws 49
Federal Guidelines on Testing and Recruitment 50

Chapter 4 Building the System: Models for the Design of Online Recruiting and Testing Systems 53

Typical Recruitment and Selection Steps and Website Components 54
Attracting Candidates through a Careers Site 55
Describing Jobs and Careers 56
Collecting Personal Information 56

Screening 57
Testing 58
Simulation-Based Assessment 58
Interviewing 59
The Hiring Decision and Beyond 60
Tracking Tools 61
Assembling the System 62
Need for Insight 62
Need to Cast a Wide Recruiting Net 63
Need for Speed 63
Candidate Commitment 63
Managing the System 64

Part II Designing and Implementing Online Staffing Systems 67

Chapter 5 Designing Online Recruiting and Screening Websites 69

Talent Acquisition: Two Disciplines 70
Tools to Support Recruitment 70
Tools to Support Screening and Selection 71
Designing Internet Recruiting Sites 72
Common Recruiting Site Components 72
Employer Overview 73
Job Information 75
Profile Matching 76
Apply Now 78
Designing Online Screening Tools 80
Resume-Centric Applicant Screening 80
Questionnaire-Based Applicant Screening 82
Common Risks Associated with Online Screening 83
Defining Basic Qualifications 85
Critical Issues to Resolve 86
When is a Job Seeker an Applicant? 86
How Detailed Should the Screening Process be? 87
How Should Applicants be Progressed through the Selection Process? 88
Summary 89

Chapter 6 Deploying Automated Tests 91

Types of Assessment Tools 91
  Assessment Content – More Than Meets the Eye 92
  Assessment Format – Something Old, Something New 94
Considerations for Using Different Types of Assessments 96
  Purpose of Assessment 97
  Program Size 97
  Job Type and Level 98
  Validation Requirements 98
  Legal Defensibility 99
  Resource Planning 100
Technology Considerations for Online Assessment 100
  Presentation of Item Content 101
  Navigation Features and Functions 101
  Examinee Instructions 102
  Testing Time 102
  Security 102
Critical Issues to Resolve 103

Chapter 7 Tracking Tools for Staffing Managers and Recruiters 105

Information for Recruiters 107
  Managing Job Requisitions 107
  Managing Candidates 109
Information for Hiring Managers 110
Information for HR Specialists 111
Critical Issues to Resolve 112
  Integration with the ATS 112
  Data Storage, Reporting, and Archiving 114
  ATS Customization vs. Configuration 115

Chapter 8 Systems Design and Integration 117

Key Elements for System Design 119
  Design Elements 119
Integration Concepts and Approaches 122
  Linking Processes – Exchanging Instructions between Systems 123

Linking Data – Exchanging Information between Systems 126
Critical Issues to Resolve 128

Part III Consequences and Issues Associated with Online Deployment 131

Chapter 9 Managing the Environment 133

Ensuring Quality in the Deployment of Online Staffing Systems 134
Issues and Challenges 135
Proctored vs. Unproctored Administration 136
Test Environment Issues 138
Technology Issues 139
Security Issues 140
Cheating 140
Unqualified Applicants 142
Access to Technology 142
The Candidate Experience 143
Strategies for Managing Online Assessment Systems 144
Summary 144

Chapter 10 Cross-Cultural Deployment 149

Adapting Talent Assessment Programs across Cultures 150
Issues and Challenges 152
Administrative Considerations 152
Measurement Quality Concerns 154
Professional Challenges 158
Technology Challenges 159
Strategies for Cross-Cultural Deployment 160
Summary 161

Chapter 11 Candidate Privacy and Data Security 163

European Data Protection Rules: A Foundational Framework 164
Design Considerations for Data and Privacy Protection 166
Notice 166
Choice 167
Onward Transfer 167

Access 168
Security 169
Data Integrity 169
Enforcement 169
Other Privacy Rules 170
Fundamentals of Internet Data Security 170
Password Protection 172
Role-Based Security 172
History and Log Files 173
Encryption 173
Additional Security Considerations 174

Chapter 12 Conclusion: The (Possible) Future of Automated Staffing **175**

Talent Supply-Chain Management 176
Evidence-Based Management 177
Network Organizations and Social Software 178
Self-Service HR 180
New Technologies to Drive Efficiency, Realism, Interest, and Engagement 181
Concluding Thoughts 182

Appendix Assessment Fundamentals **183**

Criterion-Related Validation 183
Content Validation 186
Reliability Indices 187
Measurement Scales 189
Fairness in Testing 190
Differential Prediction Analysis 191
Adverse Impact Analysis 192
Selected References for Further Reading 193

Notes 195
Name Index 203
Subject Index 205

Series Editor's Preface

The *Talent Management Essentials* series presents state-of-the-art thinking on critical talent management topics ranging from global staffing, to career pathing, to engagement, to executive staffing, to performance management, to mentoring, to real-time leadership development. Authored by leading authorities and scholars on their respective topics, each volume offers state-of-the-art thinking and the epitome of evidence-based practice. These authors bring to their books an incredible wealth of experience working with small, large, public, and private organizations, as well as keen insights into the science and best practices associated with talent management.

Written succinctly and without superfluous "fluff," this series provides powerful and practical treatments of essential talent topics critical to maximizing individual and organizational health, well-being, and effectiveness. The books, taken together, provide a comprehensive and contemporary treatment of approaches, tools, and techniques associated with Talent Management. The goal of the series is to produce focused, prescriptive volumes that translate the data- and practice-based knowledge of organizational psychology, human resources management, and organizational behavior into practical, "how to" advice for dealing with cutting-edge organizational issues and problems.

Talent Management Essentials is a comprehensive, practitioner-oriented series of "best practices" for the busy solution-oriented manager, executive, HR leader, and consultant. And, in its application of evidence-based practice, this series will also appeal to professors, executive MBA students, and graduate students in Organizational Behavior, Human Resources Management, and I/O Psychology.

Steven Rogelberg

About the Authors

Douglas H. Reynolds is the Vice President of Assessment Technology for Development Dimensions International (DDI). Doug's work is focused on the design and implementation of new behavioral and psychological assessments used for workforce selection and career development. He has designed and implemented large-scale assessments and tests with many Fortune 500 companies and several federal agencies. In the 1990s, Doug designed and developed some of the first Internet-based job application and qualification screening instruments used for large-scale corporate recruiting. More recently, his work has focused on the creation and deployment of Internet–based behavioral simulations used for executive and leadership evaluation. Doug also has served as an expert witness regarding personnel selection practices, and he has published and presented frequently on topics related to the automation of screening and testing for job selection. Prior to joining DDI in 1996, Doug worked for the Human Resources Research Organization (HumRRO) where he conducted and managed personnel research for the military and Federal agencies. Doug received his Ph.D. in 1989 from Colorado State University.

John A. Weiner is Vice President of Products and Services at PSI Services, LLC, where he is responsible for the strategic direction of PSI's assessment products and services for employee selection and development. Over a 25-year career in the assessment industry, John has led the development and implementation of sound and legally defensible instruments and systems for talent acquisition in hundreds of business and government organizations. He has worked extensively in the design and implementation of automated assessment systems, including the adaptation of cognitive ability and personality measures to online delivery, and integration among component systems. John has written numerous papers and presented frequently at national conferences on a variety of topics related to selection and assessment, including issues in technology-based assessment. He earned an MA in psychometrics in 1981 from California State University, Sacramento.

Preface

Internet technologies have introduced profound changes in many aspects of our lives. Daily activities such as shopping, planning travel or recreation, exploration of our personal interests, and even dating have all been affected. Many organizational processes are affected also: purchasing processes, supply-chain management, and customer-relationship management have been reinvented to take advantage of the new technologies. Big changes have also occurred in the way that people look for new jobs and how organizations recruit and select them for work. In many ways, Internet technologies are ideally suited for facilitating the information exchanges that start the job search–employee selection process. This book is about the new technologies that facilitate the hiring process and the best practices for effectively implementing them in talent acquisition.

The book includes three parts. First, the context and foundations for online recruiting and selection are explored. This section provides recent background on the trends that triggered dramatic changes in organizational staffing – trends that operate today. These trends can help you understand the drivers behind the new industry of HR technology as well as point you toward the factors you need to consider when making the case that your organization should invest in these tools. Background on the foundational disciplines of computer technology and psychological measurement is also reviewed at a high level in Chapters 2 and 3, respectively. Chapter 4 provides a unifying view of how these pieces fit together in the context of organizational hiring.

In the second part, the book focuses on the practical advice for designing and implementing online staffing systems. We review career portals, applicant screening and testing systems, as well as applicant tracking systems. In Chapter 8 we focus on special topics associated with systems design and integration to recognize that nearly any online process is now a configuration of separate components.

In the third part we examine several issues that anyone involved with modern staffing processes will encounter. Specifically, we review issues regarding the proper environment for deploying tests and other assessments, the implications of global access, and data security and privacy policies. For each of these areas we share advice and guidance that has worked for many organizations facing these challenges. A final chapter shares recent trends and their implications for new advancements in the field of technology-based hiring.

This book was written from the point of view of the professionals who have responsibility for systematic hiring processes, including both the recruitment of a pool of candidates and the selection of the best candidates into the organization. Often, this responsibility sits within an organization's Human Resources or Talent Management function. While many of the examples pertain to this type of role (e.g., Director of Staffing Practices, VP Talent Management, Recruiting Managers), professionals in HR Information Technology, Legal, and Marketing are frequently involved with these processes and were included in our planning for the intended audiences. We also intended students of human resources, general management, management information systems, and workplace psychology to benefit from this practical treatment as a supplement to more theoretical sources. We hope our intention is fulfilled.

In short, the goal of this book is to provide an accessible introduction to the practical aspects of implementing and operating Internet-based tools for hiring in organizations. It is not about the techniques used by single recruiters or job seekers. Many good sources exist to guide the process of posting jobs and searching for job candidates. This book focuses on the larger technology-based organizational systems that can be deployed to optimize the recruiting and staffing process.

We gratefully acknowledge the input of our clients, friends, and colleagues who worked through the early evolution of the processes described here; these professionals braved the experience of being on the bleeding edge of new technology so that others could benefit from new-found best practices. We also thank our editors and reviewers who improved upon our work in many ways. Finally we must acknowledge our generous partners: our families, for tolerating our frequent absences, and our employers, Development Dimensions International and PSI Services LLC, for providing us with the opportunity to help create the exciting world we describe here.

Douglas H. Reynolds, Pittsburgh, PA
John A. Weiner, Burbank, CA
June, 2008

Part I

The Context for Online Talent Acquisition

Chapter 1

The Context and Business Case for Technology-Based Recruitment and Selection

"The future is already here – it's just not evenly distributed"
(William Gibson)

The observation by Gibson captures the essence of the issue faced by executives and managers challenged to reshape their systems and processes to take advantage of what the latest technologies can offer: some organizations readily adopt and absorb new tools and processes and others do not. Human resources professionals feel this pressure acutely, as nearly all of the administrative and strategic functions within HR have been re-tooled to be technology-driven. The challenge for the professionals and executives in the HR function is to both understand the benefits in new technologies and to persuade the broader organization to invest in them; that is, they must build the business case for the investments and changes that will push the organization forward. This chapter provides background on the rapid evolution of the technology tools that support organizational staffing. This information should be considered when you build your business case by determining where your organization stands now and how far into the available future you desire to take your staffing activities.

The business case for technology-based recruiting and staffing processes should be tailored to the unique conditions in your organization. Consider the case of Sandra, an HR leader for a large heavy equipment manufacturer that we will refer to as XYZ Corporation. Sandra's organization currently operates with a mix of traditional and technology-based recruiting and personnel selection processes and tools; some are homegrown, others were purchased by individual plants as their needs dictated. Sandra sees an opportunity to improve her organization's effectiveness, efficiency, and strategic impact by centralizing and automating many aspects of the recruiting and staffing process, but she realizes it will take a strong push to get the company's executive team to support a big initiative. After persuading several executives that XYZ should consider the issue more seriously, Sandra was given an opportunity to present the business case to the whole executive team. When building her business case presentation, she considers the biggest challenges faced by XYZ in light of the factors that have recently influenced many other companies that have effectively implemented technology-based HR systems. In this chapter, we review these factors and follow along as Sandra builds the presentation that could change her department and have a dramatic impact on the whole of XYZ.

Driving Factors: A Brief History of HR Technology Tools

The practice of hiring new employees into large organizations has changed dramatically since the mid-1990s. This shift is due primarily to the rapid evolution of Internet-based technologies to facilitate and accelerate the staffing process. HR executives' and staffing managers' roles now include significant technology responsibilities intermixed with their accountability for recruitment, hiring, and on-boarding new employees.

As the Internet rapidly grew in size and popularity in the mid to late 1990s, organizations began to examine how the new technology could be used to their advantage. Several, but not all, traditional functions within large businesses began to remake their operational processes to take advantage of the Internet. In some organizations, the human resources functions of recruitment and selection of new employees were among the first processes to rapidly adopt the Internet as a core element of the business process. Why would the HR function be among the first adopters of these technologies; what challenges led them to design and implement them?

As is often the case with any rapid uptake of new technologies and business processes, the drivers behind the change must have clear advantages for the organizations that adopt them. Change that is driven by the advancement of new technology alone does not sustain. For technology-based recruiting and staffing, a confluence of several factors was behind the rapid development and adoption of new tools and processes: labor market conditions that constricted the supply of qualified applicants during a time of economic growth, business trends that pushed non-core activities toward automation or outside the company altogether, the development of the new electronic technologies, and the availability of scientific methodologies to collect information that will successfully predict employee effectiveness and long-term fit with the organization. Figure 1.1 summarizes these factors.

The Labor Market Context: "We Need Good People!"

The 1990s economic expansion in the United States was unusually strong compared to others in the prior fifty years; this growth period was characterized by its unprecedented length, strong growth in GDP, increased productivity, higher profitability, high rates of investment, low inflation, and low unemployment.[1] During this same time the labor market became increasingly constrained due to demographic factors such as an age gap in the population related to the fact that the post-Baby Boomer generation was smaller than its predecessor.

Extending the difficulty of the situation further, the skill level required for new jobs also has been steadily increasing. This trend

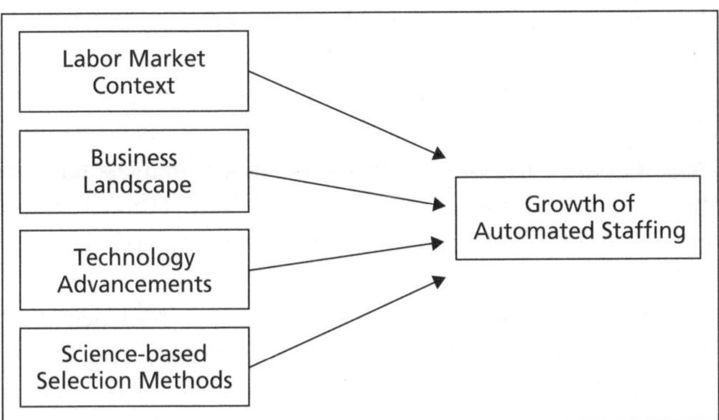

Figure 1.1 Factors affecting the rapid growth of automated staffing technologies

was widely publicized in labor market studies showing that new jobs in the United States were expected to require increasing levels of skill. One influential demographics report made dire predictions about the consequences associated with increasing skill demands for new jobs at a time when fewer people were available to take them.[2] Of course, new jobs mean new opportunities for individuals, and immigration patterns were expected to shift accordingly. The Department of Labor-sponsored report predicted that the demographics of the United States would change such that the labor base would have lower skill levels than its predecessor, largely due to demographic trends, an influx of émigrés seeking employment, and flaws in the U.S. educational system that produced graduates who lacked critical basic skills.

So as the 1990s began, the predictions for large organizations were alarming: HR leaders were to expected to staff for job growth, these new jobs were likely to be more complex and demanding than the old ones, and the available labor force would have fewer people and lower skill levels. Clearly HR leaders, and their recruiting and staffing specialists, were in for a rough ride. Successful organizations will recruit the best people for their new jobs, leaving the slower organizations fighting for the remains. In short, to sustain growth, employers were forced to become increasingly competitive for new employees to attract and hire the best people for their new jobs; the "war for talent" was under way.[3]

Many of the trends that were first described in the 1980s and 1990s have become prominent aspects of our current-day workforce and society. Demographers have charted the increased diversity of the workforce due to recent changes in immigration, educational institutions have been pressured to ensure that students develop the basic skills required for work, and businesses have been increasingly focused on innovation and change to remain competitive – thereby requiring workers to continually learn and adapt to new processes.

Sandra from XYZ Corp. considers these trends and demographic patterns as she builds her business case. She collects information on the number of retirements XYZ expects over the next few years to calculate the number of positions she will need to fill. She compares this figure with the size of the applicant pools for key roles and she notices that the number of applicants has dropped in some regions.

She interviews functional leaders about how the requirements for new positions will be likely to change in the next few years, and she asks about the importance of finding new people who have better skills and abilities than the typical applicant in the past few years. As she compiles this information into her briefing slides, Sandra begins to see how larger trends have echoed into XYZ Corp.

The Business Landscape: Shape Up or Ship Out

A second trend that evolved during this same period involved the identification of activities that could be standardized, automated, or pushed outside of large businesses. This operational philosophy can be contrasted with organizational models that emphasize vertical integration, or the assembly of all aspects of a business within the enterprise itself, such as the classic example of a steel manufacturing company that owns iron ore and coal mines as well as the means of transportation to bring these essentials to the center of production.

Also, competitive pressure to reduce fixed operating costs forced many organizations to eliminate jobs; businesses became more competitive and profitable by allocating corporate resources toward those aspects of the operation that produce a unique value in the market. That is, if routine aspects of a business operation could be standardized and automated, more resources could be devoted toward the aspects of the operation that bring the highest return. In his popular book on the globalization of business, Thomas Friedman describes how General Electric partnered with an Indian company to develop GE's software and how Simon & Schuster outsourced the digitization of manuscripts, also to India, at a substantial savings.[4]

The trend toward outsourcing of various aspects of a company's operations allows for new companies to evolve that specialize in the aspects of business that are outsourced. By aggregating the volume of work across their client base, these outsourcers are then able to drive further innovation and automation to improve operating margin and to provide cost savings to their customers. In short, companies are often not able to achieve better cost savings through improvements in their own internal operations than a third party that specializes in the function is able to achieve. This efficiency creates a market for outsourced services that are pooled across organizations.

As this trend gained momentum, the implications were felt in HR departments too, as transactional and tactical aspects of the function were standardized and outsourced. Because the HR function is not a core business, as the business trend toward outsourcing continued, so did the pressure on HR to find additional tasks that could be contracted outside the company. Benefits services, retirement programs, time tracking and payroll, outplacement services, and recruiting are just some of the frequently outsourced HR services in many large organizations.

This trend is important for understanding the broader business case for two reasons. First, by standardizing and automating tasks, organizations are better able to support them internally, thereby reducing the need to outsource them to a third party. Second, outsourcers themselves must standardize and automate these processes so that they are able drive efficiencies of scale across their clients. Outsourcing of non-value-added aspects of a business operation thereby provides an important motivator for businesses to invest in the automation of the various aspects of the HR function that we will discuss in this book.

Sandra incorporates these facts into her business case. She knows that at least one member of the executive team has proposed extensive outsourcing of the HR function as a cost-saving measure. While she does not agree that large-scale outsourcing is right for the unique culture at XYZ, she does look for ways to incorporate the concept into her proposal. For example, Sandra is aware that the company pays far too much for applicant processing services, such as background checks and health screening. These services have been contracted separately by each plant. Although she has sought proposals from outsourced service providers to take on these functions for the whole company, their proposals have been too costly – mainly due to the lack of common systems at XYZ for the outsourced process to replace, so each vendor included extra fees to create a common process for XYZ. With the executive committee's approval, she could move toward a common technology platform for the company that would allow for some staffing services to be outsourced to just one vendor. Sandra begins to feel energized at the prospect that, if they increased outsourcing and automation, her staff might be able to have more time to focus on the tasks that really matter, such as finding new recruiting channels for their toughest positions to fill.

Growth of the Internet

Perhaps most obvious of the major trends that have influenced the evolution of online recruiting and selection tools is the rapid growth and acceptance of the Internet itself. The U.S. Department of Commerce has tracked the use of the Internet through a series of longitudinal surveys beginning in 1997 and similar research has been extended by the Pew Internet and American Life Project. Their research demonstrates the meteoric rise in the usage and acceptance of the Internet as an aid to nearly any endeavor involving information. Some critical findings from this research include the fact that the pace of Internet usage was dramatic in the late 1990s and early 2000s, as shown by the dotted-line curve in Figure 1.2.

As the use of the Internet spread, so too did its application in businesses and other large organizations for the purpose of recruiting and selection activities. The solid-line curve in Figure 1.2 shows the adoption rate of online recruiting tools during the peak years of growth

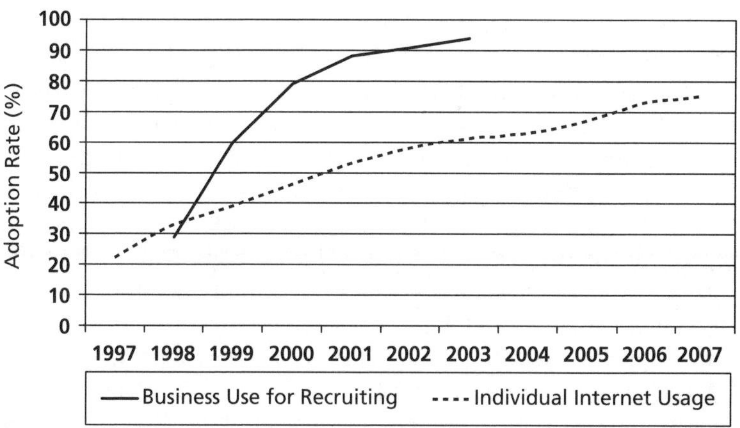

Figure 1.2 Internet adoption percentage rates, for businesses (1998–2003) and individuals (1997–2007)
Sources: iLogos, 2003; U.S. Dept. of Commerce, 2002; Pew Internet and American Life Project, 2007.

between 1998 and 2003.[5] By 2002 it was estimated that over 90% of large businesses were using the Internet for recruiting, and over 70% included user functions such as online resume submission, search for specific openings, and candidate–recruiter communications. At that time, about 35% of the surveyed companies included an online application method as the primary method of applying for jobs, and as these technologies evolved this percentage has increased.[6]

Early use of the Internet for recruiting and job application was not without risk, however. Surveys on access and use of the Internet found differences due to race, gender, and age.

This pattern sparked early concerns that, at least in the United States, we were moving toward a "digital divide," where the adoption rates may have split across demographic categories. Despite the early differences in usage rates associated with various aspects of U.S. society, these differences began to shrink very quickly. Usage rates for major demographic subgroups increased rapidly during the 1990s and early 2000s for all groups, and even faster for some groups that showed lower usage rates early on. What's more, groups that lacked at-home access were shown to be more likely to use computers and the Internet from public locations.[7]

The reasons why people use the web have also been examined, and job search has ranked high on the list. Even more important in light of the demographic differences in usage rates is the fact that minorities who use the Internet were more likely than whites to use the Internet for job search. This is a critical finding: despite early differences in at-home availability of the Internet, minority groups (on average) were more likely to get access to the Internet outside of the home and more likely to use the Internet for job search than were whites. For recruiters and staffing specialists this was an essential ingredient for the viability of online hiring tools. If the use of the Internet for recruiting and selection were to limit the inflow of diversity candidates it would raise a barrier for organizations driving toward an increasingly diverse workforce. Users and designers of Internet-based recruiting and staffing tools must still attend to issues such as differences in access rates that may limit the diversity of their applicant pools, and familiarity with the available demographic research can help inform this understanding.

Of course, the uptake of Internet-based staffing technologies in organizations was influenced by all of the trends mentioned above.

Organizations were motivated to cast a wider recruiting net because of the population demographic shifts that provided fewer qualified candidates, economic shifts that increased the skill requirements of new jobs, and business trends that pushed repetitive and transactional activities toward automation and/or outsourcing. Taken together these factors help to explain why the HR function in large organizations was among the first to adopt and innovate Internet-based business processes. The Internet is now an integral part of business functioning and a recognized and accepted way that people find jobs. Chapter 2 will explore in more detail the changes in computer and Internet technologies that have facilitated this growth.

Sandra is painfully aware of the wide availability of online tools to help staff XYZ Corp. Her competitors have systems that are far more automated and centralized than anything that XYZ has been able to put together. She considers how this could be turned to her advantage when pitching her business case: XYZ is already using the Internet for job posting and resume intake, but what happens after that point varies by location and position. The fact that so many companies invested in their online tools earlier leads Sandra to consider how they can perhaps avoid the costs and frustrations that those early-adopters often face. She decides to add a chart to her business case briefing that shows the major providers of online technologies that currently serve other organizations of a similar size to XYZ, including some of their competitors. She notes the size and tenure of the technology companies also, because she knows that some executives have raised concerns that technology providers tend to be small and unstable. As she scans over her slides she feels confident that she can make the point that the market for technology has changed since the dot-com boom and bust. Sandra also notes the job series that would most benefit from consistent online recruiting and staffing practices. Most of XYZ's sales and engineering applicants already arrive via electronic resume submissions and e-mail, so additional automation would likely be welcomed by these job seekers. However, based on information she heard from several plants, she expects that the hiring process for some of the hourly production positions will need to be different, because many of these applicants don't use resumes. The process for these jobs may also need to include a back-up process for job seekers that don't have easy access to the Internet. Despite these reservations, Sandra is confident that the executive committee will quickly acknowledge her point that the market for HR technology has much that XYZ could put to better advantage.

Science-Based Selection Methods

The fourth factor that facilitated the rapid advancement of technology-based staffing is not a new trend, but rather an extensive base of research and measurement tools that has been established for decades within the fields of applied psychology (e.g., industrial psychology and psychological measurement). The confluence of the factors described above created conditions where the needs for better methods for selecting people were more pronounced than in the past. As employers began to use the Internet as a method for accepting candidates, a new set of problems emerged: some employers were now overwhelmed by the applicant flow generated by the new procedures. Suddenly the demand increased for assessments that could be used to sort and prioritize candidates based on their responses to a web-based application blank so that recruiters didn't have to spend hours wading through the thousands of profiles that could be generated from online systems. Carefully designed screening and testing tools allowed employers to narrow their focus more quickly to just those job seekers who had the highest probability of success on the job.

Many of these measurement tools and techniques began to be incorporated into technology platforms designed to manage high-volume Internet recruiting and staffing processes. However, these assessment tools tend to add some complexity and HR professionals who invested in the new electronic recruiting and selection technologies needed to become more knowledgeable about how to determine the quality of an assessment before implementing them.

The specifics of these assessment tools and techniques, and the keys to understanding their proper implementation within technology-based staffing systems, will be elaborated throughout this book.

Sandra includes a section in her business case about the increased effectiveness of a workforce that has been selected based on well-designed and validated assessments. She finds a substantial quantity of research that shows a relationship between assessment scores and performance on jobs that are nearly identical to those at XYZ. She also realizes that she will need to be cautious about the tools she chooses to ensure they are a good fit for XYZ's processes as well as the technology systems she will consider.

The Human Resources Challenge: Better, Faster, Cheaper … and More Strategic

The four factors described above each influenced the development of what is now a broad marketplace of tools to support the automation of the recruiting and staffing processes. These tools emerged within the context of the needs of the HR professionals who must implement and support them. This context is also important to understand because it defines the ways in which automated tools can add value to organizations.

The HR function must respond to the challenges posed by the organizations they staff, and these challenges are amplified by the trends above. Like most organizational processes, the pressure to perform routine activities more effectively and at lower cost is ever present. The tools and processes described in this book were each designed to impact one or more of these challenges. If advantages were not achieved, at least in part, then new approaches became short-lived fads. The advancements described in the subsequent chapters were selected to represent those components that have had measurable and demonstrated impact on one or more of the following business challenges.

As Sandra completes her business case, she considers the pressures that she and her HR staff are under at XYZ, and she also wonders if this might also be an opportunity to demonstrate how she can add even greater value to the direction and success of the company at large.

Efficiency and Speed

The process of identifying and hiring new people is fundamentally transactional; in a typical process contact information is exchanged, resumes are collected and distributed, selection measures are administered, interviews are conducted, and hiring negotiations then commence. While these activities take place, the organization is losing time and money due to an unfilled vacated position or a new business strategy that remains unrealized because of the personnel shortage. This places pressure on the HR system to innovate toward faster cycle times for filling positions. Efficiency at each step is also critical, and efficiency can be defined in many ways. Examples include fewer HR staff hours required to perform each step, identification of candidates that won't be successful at later steps in the process (and are thus dropped from consideration), and the collection of just the right amount of information at each step to allow for effective decision-making. Each of these examples provides a motive for organizations to push toward the automation of this process. In a business environment where qualified labor can be increasingly scarce, HR executives are challenged to force improvements to the speed and efficiency of the hiring process.

Insight and Predictive Accuracy

During the course of this transactional process a critical event occurs: decisions are made about people. If the drive to improve the hiring process responds only to the business challenge of increasing efficiency and speed then an important opportunity is lost. Effective hiring processes include the collection of information to support decision-making at several steps in the process. Organizations can gain advantage to the extent that they use tools and processes that allow for deeper insight into the people they consider. These insights can support better predictions of how well the candidate will perform on the job and his or her fit with the role. Insight and accuracy can be enhanced at each stage of a hiring process, but many organizations place their emphasis on speed over quality in an effort to resolve the short-term issue of filling open positions. However, gaining insight and improving decision-making accuracy are more nuanced endeavors than gaining speed and efficiency. Without careful analysis, HR managers can be susceptible to choosing unproven techniques that promise to improve the quality of new hires. Several chapters in this book are devoted to understanding the basics of how information collected during the hiring process can be used to make better people decisions as well as faster ones.

Strategic Impact

Perhaps the most enduring and rarely achieved business challenge handed to HR professionals is the opportunity to have a strategic impact on the direction of the organization. Increasingly today's businesses must differentiate themselves in the marketplace through innovation. And, compared to earlier business conditions, a larger proportion of organizational assets are now held as intellectual property and human capital rather than as physical property such as machinery, buildings, and land.[8] This shift implies that successful organizations are those that can attract, hire, and retain the employees that add the most value to the enterprise. Employers are thus increasingly concerned with talent issues such as how skill gaps can be identified earlier and filled faster, how employees can be deployed and aligned for maximal impact, and how their culture and values can help support employee engagement and retention. In short, organizations are recognizing that their brand as an employer can be a competitive advantage – if it reflects positively to the marketplace of future and current employees.

These conditions raise the stakes for HR professionals. The rise in value of human capital assets as a proportion of company assets intensifies the scrutiny and expectations on these functions. Moving beyond tactical efficiency issues, to provide unique insight into how human assets are operating within organizations, allows HR professionals to add new value that shapes corporate strategy. Senior executives that are at the forefront of these economic dynamics are asking questions of their HR partners such as:

- How many and what sort of people do we need to take the business to the next level of growth?
- What challenges will we face as the organization competes for this talent?
- How will we deal with shortages of people and skills in the talent marketplace?

- How will the culture and values of the organization be preserved and enhanced?
- Can we identify people who will become effective strategic leaders to lead the company in the future?

To answer these questions, HR professionals require information to monitor and measure the condition of an organization's human capital. Electronic tools that provide real-time reports on applicant flow, hire rates, on-the-job performance, and similar variables are valuable to HR executives because they inform the answers to these strategic questions about the workforce.

Sandra adds some concluding points to her business case briefing that focus on the challenges that the XYZ executive committee has handed to her in recent years. She adds examples that focus on the constant pressure to improve upon the time it takes to fill open positions and to manage an increasingly complex set of information about each applicant and employee; she has also been asked to reduce costs in her area on several occasions. She includes some "what if" questions for the group: What would the value be to the VP of sales if she could identify candidates that were, on average, 10% more productive than the current sales force? What if she could select customer service reps that stayed in their roles for 20% longer than the average tenure? And, what if she could better forecast the hiring needs related to a new business strategy that the executive team is considering? Sandra also includes some questions about the risks of not acting, as she is aware of new regulations that require better tracking and reporting about applicants received via the Internet. She is increasingly concerned that XYZ's disparate systems and processes leave them exposed to some big liabilities.

Sandra wraps up her briefing slides feeling confident that the presentation will be a success. In fact, it turned out that she was even more successful than she anticipated … the executive team allocated a special short-term fund so that she could immediately begin the design and implementation of a company-wide recruiting and staffing support system. Next, her challenge is to better understand the benefits, risks, and challenges associated with all the choices she will need to make as the system takes shape.

We will check in on Sandra again in the first two parts of the book, but as we leave Sandra to her task for now, we note that her case is much the same as that of many other HR professionals. The specific factors that will help you make the case for technology investment in your organization may differ, but the trends, themes, risks, and benefits are likely to be similar to those that Sandra explored. The tips shown in the box below summarize many of the common questions that are explored when justifying a shift toward automated recruiting and staffing tools.

Good to Know:

Making Your Business Case

- What demographic patterns are at work in your organization?
- Are planned retirements increasing?
- Do you have a sufficient number of candidates for critical roles?
- What is the cost of routine manual activities in the recruiting and staffing process?
- What savings have accrued from outsourcing or automating other aspects of HR?
- How many different technology tools are used for similar purposes around your organization? Do these tools share data easily with one another?
- What is the ratio of electronic to paper-based applications for high-volume jobs?
- Are assessments used regularly to identify high-potential candidates?
- What is the value of higher performance or longer tenure for critical roles?
- Are common HR metrics such as time-to-fill and applicant-to-hire ratios tracked?
- Are data about people tracked and reported in a manner that allows for the implications of new business strategies to be readily understood?

In this first chapter we have described the context within which large organizations began to allocate millions of dollars toward improved processes for hiring their employees. These investments created a new market for HR technology tools. All of these trends and pressures were operating at a time when venture capital funding was flowing toward technology start-up companies – companies that were intent on mining new Internet technologies for meeting a great variety of needs, both real and imagined. The needs of organizations to address labor gaps were quite real, and a rapidly growing industry of technology providers emerged to create tools to address the needs. Like any industry, the pressure to differentiate was essential to the survival of these Internet start-ups. New ways to view the hiring process emerged, with a rapidly growing set of tools to drive new efficiencies and add strategic impact. This industry also moved rapidly toward consolidation, both because many smaller companies were not sustainable in the marketplace, and because consumers of these services saw value in larger combinations of tools and process over smaller stand-alone products that addressed just one aspect of the recruiting and hiring process alone. We return to this industry trend in Chapter 2 to examine how the consolidation of these technology companies has affected the market for automated staffing tools and processes.

Chapter 2

The Technology Landscape

Why do HR practitioners and executives need to know about the specifics of how technology tools operate? Some of the important reasons include:

- HR can better help to drive the strategy for the deployment of automated systems if they better understand technology issues.
- As a well-informed customer of technology, HR can understand why some things are harder than others, and can avoid asking for solutions that are unreasonable, and that add cost or complexity that is hard to maintain.
- Tech-savvy HR executives will make smarter choices about the expected impact of technology so that return on investment is maximized.
- Understanding the recent changes that have occurred with Internet technologies is important for HR managers who are deciding whether or not to build a component with in-house software engineers.
- Risks can be reduced when the customers of technology know the potential barriers. For example, the underlying architecture of a system can have implications for the functionality that can be supported and the ability to integrate across various systems.

Many of these benefits accrue because of the fact that technology is continually advancing. New development tends to progress in two ways: through continuously improving prior versions of the software or by radically revising the foundational aspects of the product or system. Managers who are less savvy and invest in a platform that is nearing the end of its continuous improvement cycle are disappointed when they learn that their new tool will require a second installation when the next version is released.

A brief look at the general models for hardware and software architecture can help ensure that investments are made with an understanding of the benefits and risks associated with the behind-the-scenes aspects of HR technologies. As you review the various models, it is important to consider how each model may be operating in your organization. Where does your information technology (IT) department stand with regard to the emerging models and trends? Why have they chosen the paths they have taken? There are usually good and strategically important reasons for the decisions they have made, and although some of these models are far from cutting-edge, many organizations deploy a variety of models to meet the needs of their business, so it is important to understand the basic ideas behind each model.

Mainframes, PCs, and Client–Server Computer Architecture

When computers were first deployed on a large scale for business applications, the hardware (the computer itself) and software (the set of instructions that run the computer) were co-located. Computers of any significant power would fill a large room. Remote terminals accessed the tool for the purpose of information input and the retrieval of the results after computations were complete, but these terminals did not hold any significant computing power or software code per se, since these aspects were associated with the central system.

The desktop computer gave rise to an alternative model whereby all of the computer's hardware and software were contained in a single unit that was manageable enough for individuals to own and operate. The popularity of the IBM Personal Computer (PC) for business purposes provided proof that this compelling new model was viable on a large scale. For these machines, software could be reduced to a user-installed and maintained product.

Although desktop systems of today are many times more powerful than the earlier mainframes, stand-alone PCs and the associated software are not without their disadvantages. The computer itself is limited in speed and power compared to larger systems within the same development era; PCs required that software be installed, maintained, and upgraded locally. So, software designed specifically for PCs was limited by what the PC of the day could handle. At first these constraints placed real limits on what could be accomplished with PC-based software. As PCs became more powerful, more software was written that stood alone on the PC.

Client–server architecture provided a balance between the mainframe and PC-based models. Under the client–server model, software was designed to run both on the local desktop machine (the "client") and a central larger system that held the core of the application on a system with higher processing capability (the "server"). This approach provided new flexibilities: software designers were able to take advantage of the speed and storage space allowed by mainframe computers while distributing local components to the desktop that could be configured to meet the requirements and role of the individual users. Client-side components could be designed to operate through easy-to-use graphical interfaces with which computer users had become familiar. An additional advantage of this model is that, because the PC is typically used as the desktop machine, the PC can play a dual role – both as a client to a server and as a stand-alone computer.

For HR staffing applications, mainframe deployments are rare, and PC-based tools have serious disadvantages when handling larger applicant or employee volumes. PC-based tools also preclude the manageable integration of data across system users. Note, however, that many "homegrown" systems may start from either of these two architectural foundations. Many organizations track applicants using spreadsheets designed for use on local machines. This approach can be cumbersome, inefficient, and error-prone, especially when applicant volume grows. However, many HR administrators are comfortable with these PC-based tools and can modify them without the assistance of a programmer, so they continue to have intuitive appeal.

The Internet Changes Everything

Just as the ubiquity of the PC drove a change in software architecture toward client–server design, the growth of the Internet had a similar influence. When software is designed to require only a web browser for the client-user, then application providers can gain the advantages of maintaining central systems that are located on servers without as much concern about how the client-side computers are configured. This also gives users and company managers who are responsible for maintaining software a variety of advantages due to the fact that, for many systems, only the web browser needs to be used and maintained on the local computers, while the service provider maintains the core of the system on their centralized servers.

As they first emerged, Internet-based technologies were intoxicating to users, developers, and investors alike. New business models and technologies bloomed and attracted large amounts of investment capital. Entrepreneurial developers raced to bring a wide variety of Internet-based tools to market. The automation of common business processes, including various HR functions, using Internet-based software began to increase rapidly. To meet the demand, many small companies emerged – each promising to provide an Internet-based service that could save labor or other routine costs.

For the HR professional, the development of these new technologies meant that the large mainframe and client–server applications that automated data-intensive functions such as payroll, benefits, time-tracking, and employee records management could be supplemented more easily with tools to support broader aspects of the process of managing data about people throughout the organization. The availability of these new Internet-based tools then placed pressure on implementers to wrestle with the difficult issue of how to integrate information from one system to the next. So, for example, candidate data collected at the point that an individual applied for a job by submitting a resume to a career site could be transferred seamlessly into the information system that tracks employee data once the candidate is hired.

The Pressure to Integrate

The need to share information across applications is not unique to HR tools. Across the range of business applications, the issue of how to feed information from one system to the next can be complex. Consider an example from Dell, where their product assembly process depends on getting the right parts from each of many suppliers in just the right quantity to meet Dell's production demand. To manage this process, Dell built a method for communicating with suppliers using web-based tools. These tools allowed both Dell and their suppliers to manage inventory in nearly a real-time manner, saving costs for all parties. In order for the process to work, it was essential that Dell's system provide information in a format that would easily integrate with each supplier's inventory management system.[1] HR processes have also become increasingly interdependent, much like Dell's production process tools. Without cross-system (and cross-company) integration, the full value of many HR systems cannot be realized.

The need to integrate tools was also fueled by larger business trends. Many Internet start-ups of the 1990s faltered as their revenue failed to grow sufficiently to cover their operating costs and investors began to grow more skeptical of the potential returns. This forced a natural consolidation, where bigger or better-resourced companies sought to add value to the market by acquiring the companies that provided tools to serve compatible and adjacent business processes.

In HR, for example, a company that provides applicant tracking software may see value in acquiring a company that provides technology that allows for resume "parsing," a process where a resume is dissected into relevant data fields such as Candidate Name and Candidate Address. If the parsing process is integrated with the tracking process, then users no longer need to manually transcribe this information into the tracking software. This process allows the company providing the tracking software to make a broader claim to the market: additional labor is saved due to the integration of the resume parsing process.

This pattern is repeated over and over in the software marketplace. Bigger, more stable, better-resourced companies seek to acquire the functions provided by companies that serve adjacent aspects of the business processes they seek to automate. Investors also follow this trend by looking for small companies that can be purchased and consolidated to deliver more value.

In the HR market, this pattern is sometimes taken to an extreme, where some software providers claim to automate the "full employee life-cycle." That is, larger software companies seek to provide end-to-end systems that manage employee information from the job seeker's first contact with the organization through his or her retirement. Sub-processes such as initial candidate attraction via a career portal, candidate assessment, on-boarding, training and ongoing development, performance management, and succession management can all be strung together as one system – as long as the relevant information in one subsystem can be transferred into another.

Although only a few software companies and their clients attempt full end-to-end integration, the integration of single components with others is a common need. Many times just two best-in-class systems will require integration to fully achieve desired efficiencies. Without integrated components, system users must refer to multiple systems, or manually enter results from one system into the next – a practice that adds labor cost and frustration to a process that is supposed to be streamlined and automated. Thus, the pressure on software providers to integrate with other vendors' tools is a frequent demand from their clients. Also, the viability of larger systems is dependent on their ability to move data between sub-components, many of which may have been developed as separate systems and then later combined.

The need to integrate across software applications has been met with a variety of tools and strategies for enhancing the integration process, and is leading to the next major revolution in software architecture and delivery.

New Integration Facilitators

In spite of the need to integrate, the design of large automated systems for handling business operations and HR functions, such as Enterprise Resource Planning (ERP) systems and Human Resource Information Systems (HRIS), has been a barrier. These huge systems evolved with their own proprietary architectural features that were designed to optimize transactions within the system, rather than between the tools and other systems. Integration in this context can be time consuming and costly.

Consider, for example, a corporation that uses a test during the selection process for customer service representatives. The test is provided by a third party that provides an online process to administer the test over the Internet. The corporation desires to have the scores from the test available and maintained in their HRIS as part of the employee's record. Typically, this integration would involve collaboration between the providers of the two systems to agree on the language used to communicate critical information, such as the test score itself, as well as the protocol for transferring the information. Software changes may also be required to facilitate the transfer and storage of the information. Furthermore, these agreements would need to be renegotiated each time a new function is integrated; so, if the corporation adds a second assessment for customer service representatives from another vendor, the process for transferring data between these systems must also be established.

Fortunately, new tools and models for integrating software systems are now emerging as a standard. Extensible Markup Language (XML) is a primary example. XML provides the basis for establishing a common language for exchanging information between systems. In the example from Dell, above, XML served as the common communication method between the various supplier systems and the hub system that was operated at Dell. Similarly, in the example where the customer service test is integrated with an HRIS, XML can facilitate the smooth transfer of information between the testing system and the HRIS to allow the company's managers to easily access results through their own system.

Another integration facilitator is Simple Object Access Protocol (SOAP) which operates as a set of instructions that can be transferred between systems. In our example, the HRIS may transfer a set of instructions to the test provider to allow access to a particular candidate and return the test score. By standardizing the language that is used between systems, the operating instructions, and many other key protocols, system integration becomes more viable than ever before. Chapter 8 describes these integration tools and processes in further detail.

The Next New Paradigm

The need to integrate software systems (among many systems or between just two) and the availability of new integration facilitators like XML are leading to whole new ways to construct software. The next emerging model, frequently described as "services-oriented architecture," treats software design as a series of components (or "services") that are internally integrated to create larger systems. The main idea behind services-oriented software is that integration is essential within an application as well as between applications. This new approach has several advantages for design efficiency and the ability to integrate across systems.

Here's an example of the benefits of this approach: At several points in the recruiting and hiring process job candidates may need to be scheduled for specific events such as telephone screening interviews, on-site assessments, and manager interviews. The software that facilitates this process might incorporate online scheduling tools that allow the candidate to pick a convenient appointment time for each event. Although the scheduling events occur at different points in the process, so that only the candidates who pass the early stages get to schedule themselves for later phases, developers using a services-oriented model would build only one scheduling component. This single component might have a few related steps and data elements, such as the ability to load available times, a calendar feature on the user interface, and a storage space in the database for the appointment times chosen by the candidates. Every time a scheduler is needed by the system, the same component is called upon to act as a service for the larger system.

This new style of software architecture is also sometimes referred to as "web services" because the approach is typically deployed over the Internet. Owing to the advantages provided by the many new tools that facilitate integration, some components of a software system can be borrowed from third parties. So, the scheduling component could be created and maintained by a separate company and simply integrated into the recruiting/hiring suite of tools whenever it is needed. Of course, if done well, this transaction is seamless and invisible to the user of the tool.

Software integration is a critical issue in the evolution of technology-based recruiting and staffing systems. Chapter 8 is devoted to this topic and describes many of the facilitating tools and processes in more detail.

The challenge for HR professionals who seek to implement and integrate these tools is to understand the technology landscape in their organizations, so that tools and processes that are a best fit within the organization can be advocated as the IT systems evolve (see the Best Practices and Realities box for a summary of the challenges involved).

Best Practices and Realities:
HR Systems Architecture and Integration

Best Practices

- System components are chosen based on their best fit for the purpose of the organization's desired HR business processes; ideal components are integrated to construct a larger system.
- HR software systems are based on current models of software architecture; they use XML and web services to integrate components within and between vendors.

Realities

- Technology-based HR systems in larger organizations are complex and shaped by their usage – new processes must often be built on top of older ones that do not integrate as easily.
- IT Departments have limited resources to devote to the redesign of operational systems, so systems that are operational may not receive attention until they are no longer functional.
- Legacy data (those that exist in current operational systems) can be a challenge to reformat and transfer into systems with newer architectural designs.
- The confluence of these realities raises barriers and challenges when implementing state-of-the-art systems – many operational systems are hybrids of new and older computer technologies.

Software Delivery Models in Transition

The way that users gain access to software systems is changing also. While there are several ways to gain access to the tools that support HR processes, three models are dominant, and these models vary in some important ways such as who hosts and maintains the system and the contractual terms related to how you pay for software (e.g., is it "rented" or owned?).

Behind the Firewall

Under this model, the software is configured for installation on the servers of the client organization's computer systems. Organizational computer systems are designed with a buffer, or "firewall," between the internal systems and those systems and networks outside the organization, thus software that is installed locally is described as being "behind the firewall." While this model is often perceived has having security advantages for processes that contain sensitive information, the benefits of this potential advantage are usually outweighed by numerous costs and inefficiencies. Having software installed within the company transfers maintenance and upgrade responsibility to the client organization, since the software provider is on the other side of the firewall.

Application Service Provider (ASP)

This configuration is sometimes referred to as a "hosted" software solution, because the software vendor hosts and maintains the software on their servers. The client organization gains access to the tool by allowing users within the company through the firewall to this destination. Two variants of the ASP model are prevalent: (a) a copy of the software is made for each of the vendor's clients so that each client has a unique instance of the tool, or (b) clients are pooled together on the same system, but their data are separated so that one company's users can't see information from another company. If well designed, the security of ASP-delivered software will be comparable to other delivery methods. The maintenance and upgrade of these systems are also far easier, because the vendor of the tool is running the system.

Software as a Service (SaaS)

This emerging model is an extension of the ASP model; however, the term "SaaS" connotes that certain elements are present. The SaaS delivery model assumes that software is fully web based – no portion is resident on the user's computer beyond the web browser. Additionally, users are pooled together on the software platform such that each client organization is sharing the same software code, although clients' information may be separated so that it cannot be viewed by other users. And, client organizations pay for a subscription to use the software and do not own or license a version of the system code. Because the tools are shared and centralized, the maintenance responsibility remains with the vendor of the system.

Technology Trends and Software Users and Buyers

These larger trends in the software industry are driving toward the inevitable conclusions that software tools are becoming increasingly integrated and reusable. What do these trends mean to those who make software purchasing decisions, HR professionals, and other users of talent management technologies? There are some common issues that arise in the course of any implementation of these tools. For example, how should the software best be configured to meet unique demands, and how will future upgrades be deployed? The way that these issues are decided will have implications for the sustainability of these technology tools.

Customization versus Configuration

There is a natural tension that arises between the needs of the users of HR software and those who develop it. Each organization's business processes will have unique needs and elements; however, the cost and complexity of software tools increase dramatically if these needs are to be met completely. Software providers that create customized solutions for their clients are often unable to realize the benefits and efficiencies from the new models of software delivery because having each client organization use a separate version of the software prevents efficiencies of scale. In the short run, this pattern can help software vendors make a sale ("we customize to your needs"), but in the long term many vendors find themselves trapped in the cost of maintaining many unique systems.

A healthier design allows for configurable options within the standard version of the product. If well designed, this allows the tool to be adjusted to the needs of users without having to copy and modify the core product each time it is deployed. This benefits the users because changes can be made easily as long as they were developed as configurable options. Software vendors benefit also because they maintain fewer versions of the software. In a true SaaS deployment model, only one version of the tool would be deployed, and all users would lease the rights to use it. Savvy purchasers of software systems will look carefully at the range of options that were designed to be configured within the tool and critically at the offer to customize features to meet specific needs.

Software Maintenance

A related issue is how the tool is maintained. No vital software tool should be static. If the tool is being actively supported, a current list of planned adjustments and upgrades should be under development at any point in time. A critical concern for those who make purchasing decisions is how these advancements are financed and deployed. If the tool has been customized to a significant degree, then the client organization may be solely responsible for funding future upgrades. If the tool is configured, then these costs are shared across the base of users. Typically users pay a fee for the continual upkeep of the system (often 15–20% of the purchase price each year the tool is in operation). In general, users will benefit when maintenance and upgrades are supported by a broad base of other users with similar needs.

Successful deployment of software tools to support organizational business processes can require a substantial investment. Aside from the financial costs of purchase and maintenance, the organizational resources required to manage the technical installation, reformulate business processes, and train users on the system can be substantial. The sustainability of the software is essential to maintain the benefits from the investment. Purchasers who carefully examine the underlying business models of their software providers can better minimize the risks due to business vulnerabilities on the part of the vendor. To the extent that vendors have a standard product, use newer technologies, and have a strong user base from which to fund maintenance and upgrades, they will have a higher likelihood of being around in future years. To be effective, HR professionals need their technology tools to become a part of the fabric of their organizations. The sustainability of an implementation should be a primary concern when investigating options.

* * *

Recall Sandra, whom we met in Chapter 1. After receiving approval from her executive team to pursue automation for the recruiting and staffing function in her department, she set out to learn more about the available technologies so she could effectively define the requirements for a system that would work well for XYZ Corp. Sandra never considered herself to be "tech-savvy," but she decided to read up on some of the latest issues and trends from an executive's perspective. (Some of her better sources are listed below.) She also met with the IT director at XYZ to discuss her developing plan; during the meeting she asks him about some of the issues she has read about. As they discuss how he applied a services-oriented approach to some of their manufacturing systems, Sandra begins to realize the IT director's growing excitement in their conversation. Toward the end of their meeting, Sandra shared a list of questions she had been developing to ask of the vendors who respond to her Request for Proposal. He suggested a few more and offered to help her with the vendor selection. After the meeting, Sandra felt a sense of accomplishment, due both to her progress toward her goal and the new partnership she felt with the IT director. Sandra's list of technology questions for the vendor selection process is shown in the box below.

Good to Know:

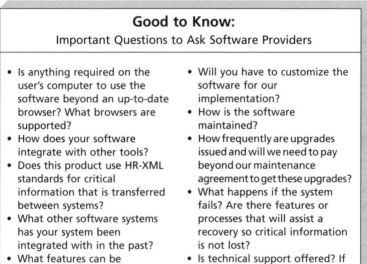

Important Questions to Ask Software Providers

- Is anything required on the user's computer to use the software beyond an up-to-date browser? What browsers are supported?
- How does your software integrate with other tools?
- Does this product use HR-XML standards for critical information that is transferred between systems?
- What other software systems has your system been integrated with in the past?
- What features can be configured to meet our needs?
- Will you have to customize the software for our implementation?
- How is the software maintained?
- How frequently are upgrades issued and will we need to pay beyond our maintenance agreement to get these upgrades?
- What happens if the system fails? Are there features or processes that will assist a recovery so critical information is not lost?
- Is technical support offered? If so, what are the costs and hours of operation?

Further Reading

Dubey, A., & Wagle, D. (2007). Delivering software as a service. *McKinsey Quarterly*, June.

Hagel, J., & Brown, J. S. (2001). Your next IT strategy. *Harvard Business Review*, October, 105–113.

Workday, Inc. (2007). *From applications to services: The shift to on-demand.* Whitepaper. Workday, Inc.

Chapter 3

Foundations for Online Assessment

Sandra needs her new online tools to assess candidate quality, as well as to generate operational efficiencies. XYZ Corporation already uses assessments for some high-volume jobs, and she is aware that these tools can be very effective. However, Sandra is also aware that she will need to be careful about how these tools are deployed when they move to an automated system. She has seen some hiring managers rely too much on assessment results while others discount the information altogether and assume that their judgment is better than an assessment. One of Sandra's goals for the new system is to use the automation in the assessment process to help standardize the use of assessments within XYZ.

At the same time, Sandra realizes that if she is going to successfully bring the assessment process online, these assessments must meet some legal and professional guidelines; otherwise they could add risk to the process. Sandra recalls studying some of these requirements for assessment in her MBA program and she decides to enhance her knowledge about how assessment can add value to her online process and about the requirements and standards for these tools. This chapter reviews what she found.

The Role of Professionally Developed Assessments

Making wise decisions in talent acquisition is crucial to the success of any organization. Management experts are quick to point out that hiring the *right* people is a key success factor for companies, helping to transform the "good to great."[1] Professionally developed assessment instruments can have a direct and positive impact upon organizations by helping to guide staffing decisions, enabling organizations to identify the best talent. Some examples of outcomes associated with the effective use of assessment tools include:

- increases in productivity, learning, job satisfaction, and customer service;
- decreases in turnover, absenteeism, theft and disruptive behavior.

How do you know when an assessment program will be effective and add value? This question should be asked of every talent acquisition program. The answer requires that you understand the essential elements of effective measurement in order to design an appropriate assessment system that is aligned with the needs and goals of your organization. Developing an understanding of basic measurement concepts will help you to build an effective talent management system, while avoiding pitfalls, such as costly "bad hires" and legal risks associated with poorly designed talent systems.

Organizations have always faced the challenge of making effective staffing decisions, from the earliest recorded B.C.-era civil service exams in China, through today's competitive quest for talent in the workforce. To be effective, it is critical that decisions be based on information that is reliable, relevant, objective, and fair. To this end, standardized assessment instruments, such as tests, surveys, and other measurement tools, are widely used as a basis for gathering and evaluating information about people to support talent decision-making.

Standardized testing and assessment are rooted in the science of psychological measurement, or *psychometrics*. This science lies at the heart of professionally developed assessments, combining elements of mathematics and inferential statistics, psychological measurement, and theories of human abilities, personality traits, and other qualities (e.g., values, interests, attitudes, performance models) to provide a method of quantifying people's capabilities and characteristics.

Psychological measurement methods are widely used in educational, clinical, and business settings. Industrial-organizational (I-O) psychologists and HR practitioners apply psychometrics to address work-related issues, such as determining job competency requirements, developing assessment instruments and procedures to measure job candidates' capabilities, and evaluating the effectiveness of assessment programs. Decades of occupational testing research indicates that properly designed measures of individual abilities, skills, personality characteristics, and work behaviors can be used to effectively predict job performance and improve hiring decisions.[2] Not surprisingly, standardized assessment instruments are widely used in systems that automate talent acquisition due to the need to make high-quality decisions about large numbers of people during the recruitment and hiring process. Valid assessments provide essential information for making these decisions.

Effective Selection of People into Organizations: Value and Risk

Assessments may be used for a variety of purposes depending upon the goals and objectives of your organization. Many types of assessments are available which can be chosen and configured to best achieve desired outcomes. When used properly, organizations have much to gain by incorporating assessments into their talent programs. At the same time, assessment users must be aware of legal requirements that apply to all employee selection practices.

Purpose of Assessment

The information collected in an assessment may be used to support a wide range of staffing processes. Common applications of assessment instruments in talent acquisition programs include: screening, selection, fit appraisal, on-boarding, development, and succession planning. Generally speaking, the size of the examinee pool and the complexity and impact of the job tend to influence the role that assessment information plays in the staffing process. For example, recruiting and selection processes for large-volume hourly jobs tend to use brief assessment tools for early stage screening, while manager and executive staffing programs tend to incorporate a more in-depth job fit appraisal, later in the staffing process. More information about typical recruitment and selection steps will be presented in more detail in Chapters 4 and 5; Chapter 6 reviews a variety of assessment instruments and their applications.

The Value of Assessment – Organizations Have Much to Gain (or Lose)

Talent assessment programs are most beneficial when they are aligned with organizational needs and goals. When establishing your assessment program, it is helpful to start by asking questions: What are the workforce concerns that the program is to address (e.g., productivity, retention, service quality, diversity)? What are desirable features and requirements of the program? What are the indicators that will be used to determine whether the program is helpful? Establishing success metrics in advance will help to ensure that the assessment program has utility and offers return on investment (ROI). Assessments that are aligned with an organization's business needs, and that meet the foundational requirements described later in this chapter, will generate stronger ROI. ROI is important for demonstrating the value of online recruiting and selection systems and is important to define early in an implementation.

A variety of approaches for evaluating ROI may be used, depending upon available resources and data. Assessment programs may be evaluated by focusing upon any important organizational outcome; these outcomes may reflect positive gains (e.g., revenue, quality, production, learning, customer satisfaction) or reducing losses and negative outcomes (e.g., inventory shrinkage, absenteeism, defects, complaints). Three basic ROI approaches are to: (1) evaluate an organization before and after implementing the assessment program; (2) compare different organization units – those that implemented the assessment program vs. those that did not; and (3) examine individual assessment results and how they are related to performance metrics.[3]

For example, pre/post-program turnover rates may be tabulated and the cost-per-lost-employee calculated to estimate the dollar value of the assessment program. The costs associated with turnover are typically estimated as a function of the time, resources, and direct costs for factors such as: separation, replacement, training, and vacancy. There are many turnover cost estimators available on the Internet, which follow similar models.[4] In addition, the U.S. Bureau of Labor Statistics is an excellent resource for information about workforce trends, including turnover.[5]

Example:
ROI

A large financial corporation used cognitive ability and work attitude tests to select approximately 2,000 candidates for entry-level service representatives in call centers located across the United States. Voluntary turnover decreased by 17% in the first 60 days, and 16% over a 180-day period, compared to the previous year, before rolling out the new testing program. Cost savings from the testing program were estimated to be $2.1 million from reduced recruitment, hiring, and training costs.

Assessment Risks

Clearly, assessments can be powerful tools for guiding HR decision-making when they are properly used. At the same time there are risks associated with the improper use of assessment instruments that warrant consideration. One potential area of risk stems from misuse and the unfortunate byproducts that it can lead to, such as misinformation about people, wasted time and resources, and mediocre or sub-par workforce quality. Ultimately these factors may impact organizational competitiveness, profitability, and growth.

Another risk is legal in nature, emanating from laws and regulatory requirements that apply to the use of employment procedures and information security. In the United States, federal agencies routinely audit the employment practices of business organizations to ensure that they are fair, job-related, and in compliance with laws and regulatory guidelines. The risk associated with litigation about recruitment and selection can be large due to the number of people who are potentially affected. For example, in 2007 a large shipping company paid over $54 million to settle a pending class action suit filed under U.S. fair employment laws, challenging the company's entire talent selection and promotion program. While the complaint was initially instigated by alleged bad behavior on the part of some hiring managers, the plaintiff's attorneys cast a wide net to examine all hiring and promotion procedures in the organization, so the scope of the suit became huge.

Professionally developed assessment instruments can also help reduce legal risks by providing an objective, defensible basis for decision-making, without which hiring-manager subjectivity can be more easily challenged. However, it is important to be aware of the fact that automated staffing systems can be used to make employment decisions, good or bad, on a very large scale, and there are inherent risks involved with decision-making processes that affect many people. Fortunately, these risks can be avoided and substantial benefits achieved through the use of sound assessment tools that possess the qualities described in the following section.

Essential Measurement Concepts

The purpose of assessment in staffing programs is to provide information to enable effective decision-making about people. In order for these decisions to be effective and useful to organizations, fair to the people who are subjected to them, and defensible to legal regulatory agencies, it is important that assessment tools possess two essential qualities: *validity* and *reliability*. In this section, we focus on these two key measurement concepts. In the next section, we provide a brief overview of professional standards and legal guidelines that apply when assessments are used in the workplace.

Validity

Validity is the most important consideration in developing and using assessment instruments. Validity can be succinctly defined as *the degree to which evidence supports the interpretation and use of assessment scores.*[6] Note that a test is not valid per se; rather, it is the interpretation and use of the test score information that has validity for a specific purpose. For example, validity evidence may support the use of scores on a personality test to predict successful performance in certain managerial competency areas (e.g., persuasive communication, managing conflict, coaching), while it may be of limited use in predicting the ability to learn in a new-hire training program for call center representatives. In this example the test may be said to have validity for selecting managers but not for selecting call center reps.

Definitions of Common Assessment Terms

- *Validity:* Evidence supporting the interpretation and use of assessment scores.
- *Reliability:* Consistency and precision of assessment scores.
- *Norms:* Assessment score summary statistics based on a reference group, used to benchmark high, average and low performance. For example, a norm group could include just managers in large companies; candidates for managerial jobs can then be compared to this norm group.
- *Percentile score:* Score below which a certain percentage of people fall; e.g., the 70th percentile is the score which 70% of examinees fall below. Percentile scores help you understand how well your candidate scored compared to a reference or norm group.
- *Cut score:* A score that is used as a decision point to select candidates to advance in the hiring process; e.g., people who achieve an interview score of 30 receive a conditional job offer.

While there are many methods for establishing validity evidence, two approaches are widely used and accepted in the professional and legal arenas: content-based validation and criterion-related validation. These approaches are described further below. One important point to keep in mind is that despite the strategy adopted, validity should be considered to be a single concept – there are not different types of validity, just different approaches to validation.

Content validation. Evidence of content validity in employment settings is established by demonstrating that the content of the assessment instrument represents important elements of the job, such as knowledge, skills, tasks, and work behaviors. The degree of match between the test and the job content is an important part of establishing content validity. The content approach to validation is ideally suited to situations where the assessment technique closely mirrors the activities and knowledge required by the job. Examples of assessments that are usually content-validated include job simulations (e.g., role playing, training simulations, in-basket exercises), skill tests (e.g., typing, office software, math), and knowledge tests designed to assess proficiency in a subject area (e.g., real estate law, mechanical engineering, sales techniques).

Content validation entails first describing the job content domain in well-defined elements of knowledge, skill, or behavior. These elements can serve as specifications for the development of the assessment. A key component of this process is the involvement of subject matter experts, such as job incumbents, managers, trainers, and other experts. These experts are enlisted to develop and review test questions to ensure that they are accurate, appropriately difficult, and representative of the target job content elements. Content validity evidence is established via this formal and systematic expert review process, which results in documented "linkages" between the content of the job and content of the assessment. This documentation of test–job element linkages, coverage of the important elements of the job content domain, qualifications of the experts, and the overall integrity of the process provide evidence of content validity. The Appendix outlines a few additional considerations for content validation.

Criterion-related validation. Evidence of criterion-related validity is established by studying the relationships between test scores or other measures (predictors) and measures of job success (criteria), such as supervisor ratings of job performance, productivity indices, sales results, customer ratings, and turnover. This validation approach is widely used for assessments that are designed to predict performance *potential*, such as tests of cognitive abilities, personality, work attitudes, biodata, and situational judgment. A measurement tool has criterion-related validity when people's scores on the tool are related to their job performance on the criteria that are studied. Under this approach, data are gathered and analyzed to determine whether people who score higher on the assessment tend to be more successful on the job. The Appendix to this book provides additional information about how to interpret the statistics that are typically used in this type of study.

If you are implementing assessments that measure abilities or traits to forecast candidates' future job success (e.g., when selecting candidates who are most likely to learn complex job tasks once they are on the job), you should ensure that the measures are supported by criterion-related validity, when it is feasible. The Appendix describes alternative strategies and considerations for conducting criterion-related studies. Many professionally developed assessment instruments are available that have been validated in a wide range of settings. This can save you the time and cost of conducting a full-scale study and enable you to leverage prior studies conducted in other organizations (see the section below on validity generalization). That said, there are benefits to conducting "local" validation studies (i.e., studies done within your organization) to optimize the assessment program to meet organizational goals and ensure that the tools are having the desired impact.

Validity generalization – leveraging accumulated wisdom. An important finding in the field of measurement is that criterion-related validity evidence can be accumulated and the overall trends summarized in a "meta-analysis," a type of study that looks at trends across several validation efforts. Meta-analyses have been conducted examining the validity of various personnel selection procedures in thousands of studies conducted over a period of several decades, spanning virtually all job families and industries comprising the U.S. labor force. The conclusions of this research are compelling:[7]

- Criterion-related validity of professionally developed selection tests and procedures holds (generalizes) across jobs, industries, and organizational settings.
- When hiring people without prior experience requirements, general mental ability (cognitive ability) is the best single predictor of job performance.
- Many other measures can contribute to the effectiveness of the selection process, such as measures of personality, integrity, structured interviews, job knowledge tests, and simulations.

The good news in validity generalization research is that organizations do not need to start with a blank slate to establish the validity of selection tests in their own settings. That is, existing validity results may be generalized or "transported" to local settings. Methods for generalizing validity results include:

- *Transportability:* Validation results for a selection procedure may be used to support its use in a new situation where the jobs are similar.

- *Synthetic/Job component validity:* Validation results for a selection procedure with respect to one or more job components may be generalized to other situations in which the job components are comparable.
- *Meta-analysis:* Criterion-related validity studies may be aggregated to best estimate the validity of a selection procedure and determine whether the results will generalize to other situations.

Importance of Local Validity

It is often prudent to gather validity evidence in support of selection tests and procedures within the organization where they will be used to:

- establish local performance standards;
- monitor the effectiveness of assessment programs in terms of local business needs and metrics;
- identify needed refinements to optimize the program (candidate flow; turnover, productivity, etc.);
- defend high-volume, high-exposure programs, especially when pass rates are relatively low for legally protected demographic groups.

Reliability

Reliability is a second essential quality that assessment instruments require in order to be effective and useful. Generally speaking, reliability is the degree of consistency, stability, and precision in measurement. The more reliable the measure, the more stable, consistent, and precise (free from error) the scores will be. Even if a test is supported by validity evidence, the degree of precision provided in the scores it produces is also important to understand and should be documented. Because no measuring device is perfect and conditions change, we expect to see at least small variations in the results when we use an instrument to measure something. The question is, how much (or little) variation are we likely to see? Knowing that, we can then decide how much variation we can tolerate for our intended use of the assessment information.

For example, you use a thermometer to take your temperature to see if you have a fever. Because the first reading is lower than you expect, you take two more readings. The temperature readings might vary slightly: 98.9, 99.1, 99.0 degrees Fahrenheit. These slight variations in the measurement of your body temperature could be due to conditions such as the position of the thermometer in your mouth, air temperature, time span between measurements, or the quality of the thermometer. The variations from these factors are what measurement specialists call "errors." Even so, you are satisfied that the results are reliable enough to conclude that you do not have a fever. On the other hand, if your temperature readings were to vary by five or ten degrees (98.9, 103.9, 93.9) you would conclude that the measurement of your temperature was not reliable enough to draw a sound conclusion about the state of your health – and you should get a new thermometer!

In the same manner, we use assessment instruments to measure certain characteristics of people and, therefore, must understand the degree of reliability that can be expected. Knowing an instrument's precision enables you to properly calibrate the level of granularity with which you interpret scores. You know that you can rely on your thermometer because when you took your temperature several times, the differences were only 0.1 degree Fahrenheit, and those differences are not large enough to be concerned about for your purposes. Similarly, you want to know that when you use a test or other assessment procedure, the scores will have sufficient consistency and precision to enable you to make effective decisions and inferences about people.

The above example illustrates one way that measurement error can affect assessment (instability). In the following sections and the Appendix, we explore key issues regarding measurement error and reliability, including:

- What are common sources of measurement error in selection tests and procedures?
- How is reliability measured?
- What should you look for when evaluating a test or assessment procedure to ensure that it is adequately reliable?

Types of Measurement Error

There are a number of potential sources of measurement error that are of concern in the use of assessment instruments and procedures. Some of the common concerns include:

- *Instability:* People are not always consistent. Changes in the characteristic that is being measured can affect scores obtained from one time to the next. For example, changes in a person's motivation can affect how they perform on some tests, and these changes can cause the reliability of the test scores to appear lower.
- *Content sampling:* Shortfalls in how the test samples from relevant behaviors, characteristics, knowledge, etc., may affect scores. For example, a knowledge test may not cover specific subject matter well enough, so that when an alternate version of the test is given, candidates tend to score differently. This limits the ability to measure the examinee's subject matter expertise.
- *Administration:* Nonstandard testing procedures, instructions, or conditions may change scores (this is a particular concern for online testing; see Chapter 9, Managing the Environment). For example, inadequate instruction to candidates may cause some to perform poorly, while unsupervised Internet-based testing may cause some candidates' scores to fluctuate.
- *Scoring.* Inaccuracies or biases in observing or scoring responses may affect scores. This is especially a concern for assessments that involve evaluators and scoring processes based on judgment (e.g., interviews, simulations).

It is important to evaluate the susceptibility of assessment instruments to potential errors in order to understand their limitations and ensure that your talent assessment program incorporates tools that are robust and effective.

Measuring Reliability

Different indices of reliability are used to describe the consistency of measurement instruments with reference to the different kinds of potential errors. *Reliability coefficients* can be derived by correlating the scores obtained in repeated administrations of an instrument to a group of people under different conditions; for example, across time, across alternate forms, across items, or across assessors (raters).

What constitutes good reliability in a test? Reliability coefficients can range from 0 to 1.0. It is generally accepted that reliability coefficients as low as .60 or .70 can be useful, especially when multiple measures are combined into a total score. At the same time, values above .90 are desirable for applications where fine-grained comparisons between people are to be made on some measured characteristic. More information about the ways that reliability can be estimated is provided in the Appendix.

Score Interpretation

Assessment instruments produce scores, but how do we interpret them? What is it that makes scores meaningful? How do we know when a score is good or bad? In this section, we explore measurement concepts that will help you make sense of assessment results.

Two general frameworks for interpreting test scores are prevalent: *norm-referenced* and *domain-referenced* measurement.[8] Norm-reference tests derive their meaning by comparing scores to a reference group (e.g., entry-level sales managers), and are typically used to compare and differentiate among people. The range of scores obtained by the reference group constitutes the norm, serving as a benchmark for comparison. Domain-referenced tests derive their meaning by evaluating how much of the test content is mastered. That is, test items are keyed to specific content elements and proficiency is defined with respect to how much of the test content the test taker has mastered. Classroom tests are the most common example of a domain-referenced test, where scores are often based on the percent of the total number of questions that were answered correctly. With a domain-referenced test, comparison to other people is not required to define performance. In personnel selection, most assessment instruments and procedures are norm-referenced. On the other hand, certification, licensure, and educational achievement tests are predominantly domain-referenced.

Norms – it's all relative. Widely used in personnel selection and development, measures of characteristics such as cognitive ability, personality traits, attitudes, biographical data, and other characteristics, are norm-referenced. The scores they produce are not meaningful per se; they gain their meaning through comparison with results obtained by a relevant reference group. Like a yardstick, they provide an objective quantification of some attribute. The yardstick measures a person's height, but does not tell us whether the person is tall or average height. Knowing that a job candidate obtained a score of 45 on a test of *problem solving ability* does not tell us whether the candidate is highly adept or marginally capable. Normative information is needed to guide interpretation of attribute measures so that we can know, for example, that a score of 45 is better than 90% of all of the people who have taken the test.

A key concept in understanding and using a norm-referenced test is the *score distribution*. When we take measurements of an attribute on a large number of people, they will typically differ. Some people will possess more of the attribute than others. When we tabulate the measurements in a chart or graph, we observe that a pattern emerges: a large concentration of people will almost inevitably score in close proximity to one another – this is what defines the average or normal score range; smaller numbers of people tend to obtain extreme scores above or below the average.

Assessment instruments differ widely in the score distributions that they yield. Many instruments are purposely constructed to produce a wide range of scores forming a nearly bell-shaped curve so that people are spread out on the measured attribute and meaningful distinctions can be made throughout a wide range of scores, such as Figure 3.1. Other instruments may produce a narrow range of scores and may be useful only for distinguishing a narrow range of attribute

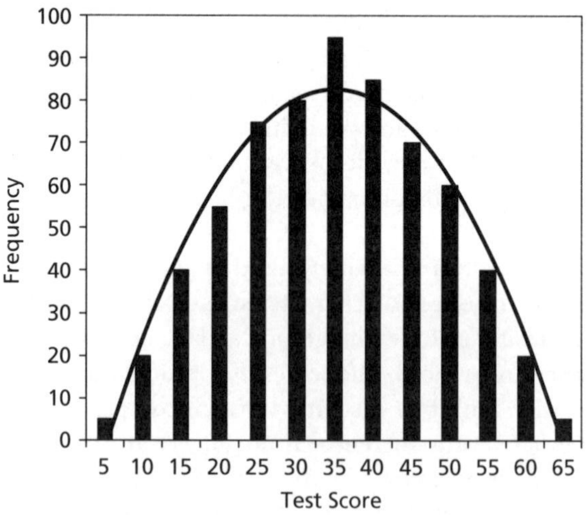

Figure 3.1 Example test score distribution

levels. Some instruments may "run out of room" in distinguishing between people and have a "ceiling effect" because they are too easy and most people get very high scores (or a "floor effect" if they are too difficult and most people get low scores). Clearly, it is important to understand the score distribution properties of a measurement instrument to ensure that it will serve the needs of your talent selection program.

Cut scores. When we say that assessments help in making good talent decisions, it implies that we will be using cut scores to make distinctions between people; e.g., to determine who will receive a job, promotion, training, or developmental opportunity. Establishing a cut score is one of the most important elements in the use of assessment procedures. When cut scores are set too low, there will be little value or utility in the assessment. *Why use the assessment if virtually everyone passes?* When cut scores are set too high, the assessment may act as a barrier (few people pass), preventing you from meeting your staffing goals. Jobs go unfilled, and the organization loses productivity and sales opportunities. And if the cut score results in a substantially lower pass rate for a legally protected group, in the United States you may be subject to a legal challenge requiring you to defend your selection program (as described in the following section). The key is to establish a job-related basis for a cut score that balances your need to be selective enough to make the assessment useful, while allowing staffing goals to be met.

Suggested references for further reading about cut scores are provided in the Appendix, and several essential considerations are outlined below.

- *What are the requirements and impact of the job?* Difficult, complex, and demanding jobs, and jobs for which safety and trust are at risk will require a higher level of aptitude (a higher cut score) than low skill, low impact jobs.
- *How selective can you afford to be?* Examine alternative cut scores, estimate what the pass rate will be in your applicant pool, and find a score that results in an acceptable pass rate to meet your staffing needs.
- *How do job incumbents perform on the assessment?* Examine alternative cut scores, estimate what the pass rate would be for incumbents

in your workforce, and identify a score that is consistent with expectations for the job. Administering the assessment to a sample of job incumbents is one way to benchmark the assessment, or norms may be published for similar jobs if a commercial assessment is used.

Professional Practice Standards and Legal Considerations

Published technical standards play a critical role in guiding professional practice and serve as a framework both for ensuring the effectiveness of assessment instruments and in meeting legal requirements for fair and job-related selection procedures. U.S. fair employment laws and regulatory guidelines require employers to avoid unfair selection practices. They also raise the stakes for employers who must make talent management decisions. It is interesting to note that that under the legal definition, a selection procedure is *unfair* when a protected group (e.g., age, gender, race, ethnicity) tends to score lower on the selection procedure, but the group performs as well as others on the job. For further discussion and technical details about test fairness, please refer to the Appendix. A brief overview of assessment standards and regulations is presented below.

Professional Standards and Principles

Professional best practices in measurement and personnel selection are guided by standards and principles established by psychological and educational associations. Two principal documents are published in the United States which generally govern good practice, and which are given deference by legal authorities in determining whether selection programs are technically sound.

Standards for educational and psychological testing. The *Standards* serve as the authoritative reference to guide the evaluation of the technical quality of assessment instruments and their use. Authored jointly by the American Educational Research Association, American Psychological Association, and National Council on Measurement in Education,[9] the *Standards* represent the consensus of the scientific community with regard to broad measurement issues such as validity, reliability, norms, and fairness.

Principles for the validation and use of personnel selection procedures. The *Principles* translate key issues addressed in the *Standards* into specific applications in employee selection and assessment. Published by the Society for Industrial and Organizational Psychology,[10] the *Principles* represent the general consensus of Industrial-Organizational psychologists and other assessment professionals regarding the practical issues and considerations when establishing valid and reliable selection procedures, and when making decisions based on these procedures.

An additional document that may be helpful to online test users is the *International Guidelines on Computer-Based and Internet Delivered Testing*, published by the International Test Commission.[11] This document is focuses specifically on considerations for development, administration, and use of assessments via computer and Internet technology.

Fair Employment Laws

U.S. federal fair employment laws prohibit discrimination in the workplace. During a thirty-year period, between 1964 and 1991, several key civil rights laws have been enacted, including

Title VII of the Civil Rights Act of 1964[12] that prohibits discrimination by covered employers (fifteen or more employees) on the basis of race, color, religion, sex, or national origin. Title VII is enforced by the federal Equal Employment Opportunity Commission (EEOC); state fair employment practices agencies may also enforce Title VII.

Age Discrimination in Employment Act of 1967.[13] The ADEA prohibits covered employers (twenty or more employees) from discriminating against persons forty years of age or older, when making hiring, promotion, termination, or pay decisions.

Americans with Disabilities Act of 1990.[14] Title I of the ADA prohibits employment discrimination against a qualified person with a disability. Covered employers include those with fifteen or more employees. A disability is "... a physical or mental impairment that substantially limits a major life activity." Employers are restricted in asking questions about medical conditions pre job offer. ADA accommodation requests are considered on a case-by-case basis.

Civil Rights Act of 1991. This act modifies some of the basic provisions of federal law in employment discrimination cases, including the right to jury trial on discrimination claims and introduced the possibility of emotional distress damages, while limiting the amount that a jury could award.

State laws. Many states have fair employment laws, and other statues that apply to assessment instruments.

Federal Guidelines on Testing and Recruitment

Uniform guidelines on employee selection procedures (1978). The *Guidelines* were published to provide employers and users of selection procedures with advice on legal requirements and criteria for the use and documentation of employee selection procedures. The *Guidelines,* published jointly by the U.S. Equal Opportunity Commission, Civil Service Commission, Department of Justice, and Department of Labor, reflect the views on test validation and use that were prevalent at the time, but do not reflect advances in test validation methodologies and findings, nor do they reflect role of technology in the advancement of assessment.[15]

Internet applicant rule (2005). The Office of Federal Contract Compliance Programs (OFCCP) issued the Internet applicant rule (added to 41 CFR 60-1.3) which clarifies the definition of a job applicant as it relates to those who apply over the Internet or related technologies. This rule also sets forth requirements for demographic record keeping for adverse impact analyses when some job seekers apply for openings using the Internet (see Chapter 5 for more information).

* * *

After her review of some of the basics about assessment, Sandra is confident that assessments will play an important role in XYZ Corporation's new automated recruiting and staffing system. From her point of view, she understands that to meet the various guidelines assessments should be validated, fair, and carefully documented. Sandra documents her key requirements for assessments in a checklist similar to the one shown below. She also arranges to consult with an assessment expert as the system is configured for the needs of her company.

Checklist for Assessment

Assessments can sometimes be complex, but some basic rules of thumb apply. Consider the list below as you are choosing assessments for your online staffing system:

- Purpose and goals: Determine why and how the assessment will be used.
- Documented validation evidence: Ensure that there is technical documentation of validity that supports the assessment for your intended application.
- Documented reliability: Ensure that assessment scores are precise enough to support your staffing decisions.
- User documentation: There should be clear written guidance for how the test is to be administered and interpreted.
- Plan for validation in your organization: Adopt a strategy that meets your organization's needs with respect to budget, measuring ROI, and legal defensibility.
- Applicant flow: Consider the potential impact of the assessment on applicant pass rates, particularly with respect to workforce diversity. Pilot studies are useful to examine the impact of a new assessment on pass rates, enabling you to make adjustments to achieve a desired pass rate.
- Consistency with relevant standards and regulations: Work with an expert to ensure that your system is documented to comport with professional testing standards and legal guidelines on employee selection procedures.

Chapter 4

Building the System: Models for the Design of Online Recruiting and Testing Systems

HR professionals are increasingly called upon to assemble software-supported systems for facilitating people processes in organizations. Beyond the design of individual software components, the issue examined in this chapter is how these components should be assembled to drive business results.

A critical question that must be addressed as technology components are chosen and implemented is how to put the various pieces together into a system that works for your business purposes. In the best online staffing systems the tools used are not stand-alone events, but rather they are strung together into a system that optimizes business outcomes. In this chapter we present design concepts for assembling assessment and technology tools into larger systems.

In short, how should HR professionals configure the larger process in which online assessment tools operate?

Many configurations of the available tools are possible and beneficial in an organization's selection process; the choice of components, and the order of these within a system, should be driven by the needs and business conditions faced by the organization. Returning to the concepts we discussed in Chapter 1, the fundamental considerations involve the underlying drivers of efficiency, cost savings, insight, and strategic value. The key to unlocking these benefits is in understanding the employee recruitment and selection process as a *system*, rather than just sequential components.

The idea that staffing components operate as a system involves understanding how a change in one area impacts other areas. For example, the methods of recruitment may influence the characteristics of an applicant pool and thus influence the percentage of people who pass a test that is administered later in the process. Another implication of taking a systems view of the selection process is that each element in the system adds something important to the result. For example, each step may target different competencies or abilities, so that the successful candidates have demonstrated at least a basic level of competence on a range of job-relevant characteristics by the time they have completed the full selection process. A systems view also implies that well-designed components can be adjusted so the system can adapt to a variety of business conditions (e.g., changes in applicant quality due to fluctuating economic conditions). A case summary of how one organization designed their online recruiting system is provided in the box below.

One of the most important considerations when constructing online staffing systems is the choice of the components that are used to make up the steps in the system. How many steps are included, and the specific tools that are used in each step, should meet the requirements of the business and should fit within the expectations of the applicant population with regard to the time commitment and effort involved. Common examples of the assessment tools and steps that are used in online systems are discussed further in the next section.

Typical Recruitment and Selection Steps and Website Components

When the recruitment and selection process is assembled into a system that is to be deployed through the Internet, a common set of steps for job seekers to follow are typically included. These steps are usually presented across several website components. The most frequently used include those described here. Each of these steps will also be discussed in more detail in later chapters; this chapter introduces these components as the job seeker sees them to show how they can be pulled together as a cohesive system. Later chapters discuss these tools from the perspective of the designers and users of the tools within the hiring organization.

Case Scenario:
An Online Professional Hiring Process

An automobile manufacturer facing a challenging recruiting market for their entry-level professional staff (e.g., MBAs, engineering, and finance) designed an online process for attracting and prioritizing top applicants. Starting from their "careers" page on the corporate website, the company first provided video testimonials from senior executives and recently hired professionals that gave an engaging and realistic view of the opportunities and unique culture in the organization. Interested job seekers were then able to search for job openings that best fit their desired job characteristics, professional interests, and work background. Job descriptions were provided for each open position that included realistic information about the nature of the role. Job seekers could then apply for the jobs they desired by completing a brief personal background questionnaire that incorporated structured questions about their education and work history as well as biographical questions that had been validated as predictors of early-career success for professional roles in the company.

This process achieved several business objectives for the company. First, the process was easily available to top candidates from around the world. Second, interested job seekers were directed to complete the profile on the website so that a common process was followed for all. Third, recruiters were able to identify the highest-potential applicants from the process to invite to more costly on-site events, where candidates participated in assessment exercises, met with executives regarding careers with the company, and completed in-person interviews. Fourth, data were maintained regarding the job seekers' interests, so that if their top-choice jobs were not available, valuable candidates could still be courted for secondary opportunities.

Attracting Candidates through a Careers Site

A careers site is a portion of the organization's primary website where job seekers may explore employment options with the company. This component is usually presented under a link on the top page that is labeled as "Careers." This portion of the site holds all of the subsequent website components that support the online recruitment process.

The highest level of the careers site (i.e., the first web page that job seekers see after clicking the "careers" link) is important for making a good first impression as a potential employer. Often titled "About our Company," this page should clearly reflect the company's brand as an employer, and include sections regarding the company culture, major benefits and flexibilities available to employees, testimonials from employees, and a clear statement about the meaning of work within the organization (e.g., a defense contractor may emphasize that employees are contributing to national security). While some companies may skip this employment branding opportunity and direct job seekers immediately to available job openings, this approach can put the employer at a disadvantage when competing for labor because it implies that the employer does not consider their employee culture to be strong enough to advertise.

Describing Jobs and Careers

Next, job seekers are directed toward information about job families, career tracks, and available positions. For many organizations, this part of the website is often supported by third-party providers that offer online recruitment tools. Job seekers are seamlessly transferred to these pages that are built to look exactly like the corporate site from which the seeker was just transported. Third-party tracking and job posting tools are often used at this point due to the complexity of the database operations involved – full-featured tools allow for many actions to be managed as positions are opened and later closed throughout the breadth of the organization's operations. These features will be explored in more detail in Chapter 5.

The jobs and careers page will have several subcomponents. Here major jobs families are described and basic qualifications for jobs are listed. Tools that allow job seekers to evaluate whether they would enjoy the work, such as a job preview, can also be positioned at this point, to educate job seekers before they choose to become applicants for the roles. Here again, the specific issues associated with the design of these tools are presented in Chapter 5. Most importantly, the jobs and careers page will also allow for candidates to search a database of open positions, review descriptions of each position, and formally enter the selection process by clicking a link or button that is usually labeled "Apply Now."

Collecting Personal Information

Next, candidates are asked for identifying information. Frequently name, address, e-mail, and/or phone numbers are requested. Some systems allow for job seekers to create an anonymous profile that only they can access until they are ready to have their profile considered for the first stage of employment screening, but at that point some type of contact information is provided. Another variant of this stage simply has the job seeker paste a resume into the system. Regardless of the methodology, at some point in the process the job seeker must submit information that uniquely identifies them. This information, and any additional data that is associated with these personal identifiers, falls under various legal and regulatory privacy guidelines that will be considered in later chapters.

Screening

Job seekers then complete questions that inquire about basic qualifications (such as certifications or licenses required by the work), relevant past experience, specific occupational skills, and other job-relevant characteristics. At this point in the process the questions should focus on the information necessary to determine if the job seeker is qualified to be an applicant for the role. Additional questions may be included that allow the qualified applicants to be prioritized for further consideration. In-depth questions, psychometric tests of ability or personality, or lengthy assessments should be avoided at this point in the process because they can put off job seekers who may have only a casual interest in the job at this point in the process. In most cases, personal information and the necessary data for screening job seekers into a qualified applicant pool should be possible to collect in twenty minutes or less.

Once the screening profile is complete, most available systems can apply pre-configured scoring rules to the responses. Job seekers who complete the full profile can then be categorized into qualified applicants and disqualified job seekers. Among those who are qualified, those with the highest likelihood of success on the job can be forwarded quickly (and in some cases, automatically) to the next phase of the selection system. Less sophisticated systems will accomplish the same screening function by having a recruiter review the responses from the screening questions, or the detail from a pasted resume, and make similar judgments regarding the next step in the process for each candidate. Chapter 5 is focused on the construction and deployment of effective screening tools. Because screening questions operate as selection tools, all of the principles described in Chapter 3 (e.g., reliability and validity) apply when considering their effectiveness as measurement tools.

Testing

Usually screening questions alone do not provide enough depth of insight to ascertain an accurate view of applicant capability and fit with a role. Although good screening questions can tell you whether an applicant has basic qualifications and experiences that may be critical for the role, this information tells you little about the quality of the applicant's experience nor does it give a strong basis for understanding their strengths and weaknesses. Going beyond the information collected during the screening phase, greater insight into individual characteristics can be achieved by deploying psychometric tests and inventories that can provide more accurate measurement. Psychometric tests are best suited for assessing abilities, traits, acquired skills, and knowledge. Aside from the tests themselves, many testing systems also routinely collect reactions from test takers regarding the ease of use and perceived fairness of the process. This information is valuable when planning for future changes to the process.

Tests can be positioned at several points in the hiring process. Because they are usually relatively inexpensive to deploy, tests are often used just after the screening phase of a hiring process. When tests are positioned early in the hiring process recruiters and managers can gain a sense of the applicants' potential for success on the job before they expend more time and money on face-to-face evaluations of the candidate. Alternatively, tests can be used later in the process to collect information that is used in conjunction with the results from other assessments and interviews. However, this model is more expensive to operate, because a larger portion of the applicant pool is evaluated by this broader set of tools. Chapter 6 provides a closer look at the choices available for online tests.

Simulation-Based Assessment

The later phases of a hiring process typically involve richer and more personal forms of evaluation. Technology tools play an important role in the deployment of these tools, and there are many options for

Assembling the System

Once staffing system designers have determined which of the staffing steps are most appropriate, these components should be arranged into a staffing system. Figure 4.1 shows how the components described above can be connected to form a larger process. Several guiding principles apply when constructing multi-phase processes such as the one shown in the figure.

Need for Insight

One of the biggest considerations when designing recruiting and selection systems is the level of insight into job candidates that is required to make sound business decisions. For some roles, where the applicant volume is high, the average rate of success is high (that is, most applicants will naturally succeed on the job), and the cost to replace a poorly performing or dissatisfied employee is low, then a minimal level of insight may be required to make a good hiring decision – this is true because almost anybody you hire will be likely to succeed, and if they don't, they are easy to replace. Conversely, when applicants are harder to find, the job is more complex so fewer can-

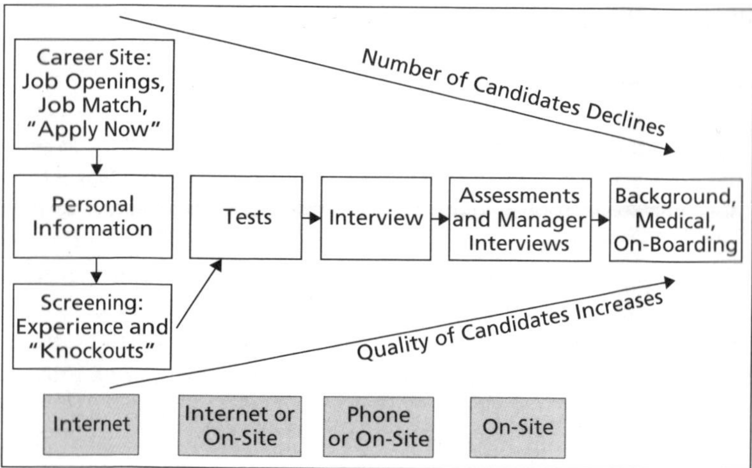

Figure 4.1 A typical job candidate flow model

configuring them to work within the hiring process. Beyond screening and testing tools, richer assessment options include simulations of work activities that will be critical for the candidate to perform if they are given the job.

For example, various call center tasks can be simulated such as handling a message from an irate customer; these simulations can be automated by presenting the customer's question as an e-mail and having the candidate choose a response from a set of options or having the candidate record or type their response to the situation for later review. For higher-level jobs, candidates for executive positions may run a simulated company for a day. In these simulations, the candidate might review and send messages, hold meetings with subordinates (who are portrayed by trained role players), and create business outputs such as analyses and presentations. All of these actions are tracked by the technology tools and are then available for later review by trained assessors who prepare a detailed assessment report. This form of assessment can give insight into critical job competencies such as a candidate's demonstrated ability to plan and organize, communicate strategic vision, analyze business problems, and handle sensitive personnel issues with subordinates. Screening tools and ability tests may also relate to these capabilities, but simulations allow you to see whether the candidates can perform these actions directly. Of course, simulated assessments of this nature can be costly, so hiring systems that use them often include careful screening and testing before a candidate is invited to participate. We will return to these forms of assessment in our discussion of the trends that are shaping the future of technology-based staffing tools in the final chapter of the book.

Interviewing

The interview is a ubiquitous selection technique. And, without knowing the damage they are causing, most hiring managers have been using the least valid form of interviewing. A consistent and well-researched finding in workplace psychology is that informal and unstructured interviews are among the least predictive methodologies for predicting future job performance.[1] There are many reasons for this finding. Many unstructured interviews lack job relevance because hiring managers are left on their own to create interview questions. Another prominent flaw is that human beings have a tendency to view other people more positively when they share common traits and experiences – regardless of whether or not these traits and experiences have any relationship to what the job requires. To make matters worse, hiring managers inflate their perceptions of their own effectiveness at interviewing and hiring. This perception is reinforced by another natural feature of our thought processes: that is, we remember our successes better than our failures, and, in fact, we can never witness some of the worst failures – those candidates who would have outperformed the person that was given the job.[2]

Fortunately, research has also shown that as consistency and structure are added to the interview, better outcomes can be achieved.[3] Various technology tools have thus been developed to help to structure and facilitate the interviewing process. These tools usually allow for the identification of the areas to be assessed (e.g., competencies, past behaviors), the construction or identification of questions that measure these areas, the assignment of questions across multiple interviewers, and a process for data combination across interviewers to help with decision-making. Furthermore, the tools can help with records retention, if the interview protocol and summary notes and ratings are maintained in the electronic system. Many of these tools are geared toward improving the efficiency and standardization of the interview process; if the tool is based on an interview technique that has been well researched and proven, additional insight into candidates and better hiring decisions can be achieved.

The Hiring Decision and Beyond

Having substantial information about candidates, through screening, testing, assessment, and interviewing, does not get you the right person in the job until the hiring manager makes the decision to hire the most-qualified candidate. Here again, technology tools have been developed to support the process. Decision support can take several forms. Common examples include automated databases that record each candidate's standing on all of the tools that were used in the hiring process. System designers, often with the help of a measurement specialist such as a workplace psychologist, can also configure

automatic decision rules that keep qualified candidates moving through the selection process. Candidates that reach the final phase have a complete set of information available in the system, and may have an automatically generated recommendation to hire or not. Ideally, these recommendations are based on statistical models that can be generated at the time the tools are validated.

Once a well-qualified candidate has been identified, many organizations continue their due diligence on the top candidate, by conducting reference checks, background investigations, and/or medical screening. Here again, the applicant tracking system plays an important role in tracking the results from these steps.

Even after the candidate is hired, the information collected in the hiring process can still be used to benefit the new hire and the organization. These benefits were often overlooked until technology tools were developed to help with data storage and reporting. For example, during the on-boarding process (i.e., the first couple of months that the new hire is on the job), information from the hiring process can be summarized for the new hire to help the manager understand where learning can be accelerated because of new hire strengths, where the new hire needs extra support and guidance due to gaps in skill or experience, and thus where planned development should be focused. These activities are triggered by reports generated from online tools that gather and store assessment results as job candidates progress through the hiring process.

Tracking Tools

Underlying each of these components is typically a backbone system that tracks, stores, and reports upon selection system data. These tools, known as applicant tracking systems (ATSs), provide a vehicle for maintaining the abundance of information that is generated by the hiring process. A well-designed ATS will collect and maintain information on candidates, positions, and selection processes to enable the efficient management of the recruiting and staffing functions. ATSs may also integrate job posting and background check services to further extend the value they provide to the hiring process through automation. Chapter 7 reviews the issues associated with implementing tracking systems to support hiring processes.

didates are likely to excel in the role, and the cost of failure is high, then a deeper level of insight into candidates for the role should be developed before decisions are made.

As the need for insight increases, the selection process can support more steps, each providing a different view into relevant aspects of candidate experience, traits, abilities, and competencies.

Need to Cast a Wide Recruiting Net

Factors such as the scarcity of qualified job seekers, uniqueness of the job qualifications, and the geographic distribution of the jobs for which applicants are being sought will each influence the need to widely broadcast information about the job. These conditions were prevalent in the late 1990s and led to the strong interest in the use of the Internet for recruiting in the first place. To the extent that these factors are present for a given job, the pressure to have at least the first few stages of a selection process online will be greater.

Need for Speed

The total time it takes between when a job is posted and when the new hire starts work is a critical diagnostic for gauging recruiting and staffing effectiveness. Speed-to-hire is usually a big concern for the hiring manager. The use of automated tools will tend to increase overall efficiency and decrease time-to-hire metrics, but this benefit should always be considered in light of other needs as well. Frequently, the need to fill a vacant role will mitigate the need to gain appropriate levels of insight into the available candidates. If a proper balance is not found between these factors, the organization risks selecting a candidate with poor fit for the role.

Candidate Commitment

Each of the organizational needs described above must also be weighed with the needs of the job seekers and their willingness to participate in each phase of the process. Here again, as the risks increase for the organization, candidates tend to understand and respect the need to obtain a deeper level of insight during the selection process. For example, candidates for executive roles often understand and respect an organization's need for a thorough assessment process; candidates for an hourly role may not tolerate more than an hour or two of evaluation, especially if they have options with other potential employers.

Managing the System

A final set of issues that must be decided as the system is developed relates to how the system is managed – in terms of the rules that are used when moving applicants through the system and the adjustments that are made to the system to accommodate changes in the business environment.

An important rule that should be determined for the system is whether (a) all applicants will be asked take each assessment in the process before a final decision is made, or (b) only those applicants who pass the assessments in earlier steps complete the subsequent ones. The first of these options is often called a "compensatory" selection process, because excellent performance in some areas of the assessment can compensate for lesser performance in others. Because the applicants participate in all the steps, it is possible to see how they stack up on all of the tools that are used. The second option is often called a "multiple hurdle" selection process, because applicants that don't make it through earlier steps are not invited to the later steps. The major advantages of each approach should be considered as a system is initially configured; however, flexible technology tools will allow for some changes to these choices as the system operates.

The primary advantage for a compensatory approach is that it provides the most information on a pool of candidates. When the stakes are high for a job selection process, this design is often best. It allows for a broad range of inputs to be considered on a larger number of job candidates by the employer before the final selection decision is made. Another advantage to this approach is the perceived fairness of providing all assessments to the candidates before anybody is rejected. The downside, of course, is the time and the cost of administering the process. If all candidates must take all of the assessments, this adds a substantial amount of time to the process and the cost of each assessment step increases because more people participate in each step compared to the multiple-hurdle model. Using the model shown in Figure 4.1, a compensatory process would allow all applicants to progress through to the stage of the final selection decision, so information from each step is available to the decision-maker before a final choice is made.

A multiple-hurdle system operates more efficiently. Candidates are chosen to participate in each assessment step based on their performance on the prior step in the process. This allows system designers to place lower cost tools at the beginning of a process, and tools that provide greater depth of insight, usually at a higher cost and bigger time commitment, in later steps. Because they have the potential to affect the largest number of job applicants, it is important that the tools used early in the process focus on critical job requirements and be highly predictive of success on the job. But, multiple-hurdle systems by definition involve making some rejection decisions based only on the information that is available at a specific point in the process. That is, some job applicants will be disqualified before they complete each possible phase of the process, so decisions made earlier in the process are made with less information than decisions that are made later in the process. Multiple-hurdle systems are also referred to as non-compensatory because poor performance on one portion of the process can't be compensated – the candidate who fails a component is dropped out of the process. If the model shown in Figure 4.1 were designed as a multiple-hurdle system, some candidates would be rejected at each of the selection steps.

In practice, most systems are neither strictly compensatory nor multiple hurdle; rather, combinations of these principles are used such that candidates might participate in early screening and testing steps, and those who pass are moved into more extensive assessments that are considered in a compensatory manner.

Once the components are arranged into a system, adjustments to the components can be made to accommodate shifts in labor market conditions that can affect the number of candidates available, as well as their quality and fit with the target role. For example, pass rates at each phase of a multiple-hurdle system design can be modified to allow a smaller percentage of applicants to progress into later phases of a selection process when the labor market is rich with candidates. By raising quality standards in the earlier steps, organizations can operate the later components more efficiently, because only the candidates with the highest probability of success are allowed to pass into the final stages. When labor markets are tighter, these pass rates can be lowered to allow for more choice in the later stages. Similarly, in a compensatory system the weight placed on the results from each component can be adjusted when a final decision is made. Instead of restricting candidate flow, these adjustments may instead be focused on putting the most weight on the components that are the most predictive of success on the job as shown through validation research on the system.

The principles associated with effective selection systems should be supported by the technology tools that make up the system. Common features include the ability to adjust scoring standards, the weight of the various components in the process, and reports that allow users to examine the effects of changes. Because these adjustments can require sophistication in measurement, and they may potentially affect many hundreds of people, security rights should restrict access to the tools that allow adjustments to pass rates and component weights so that only qualified users are able to make these changes.

In the first section of this book we have examined the foundations of technology-based recruitment and selection. In the next section we build upon this foundation to provide practical detail regarding the implementation of various aspects of technology-driven staffing processes.

Part II

Designing and Implementing Online Staffing Systems

Chapter 5

Designing Online Recruiting and Screening Websites

Sandra from XYZ Corp. considers her options as she plans for the design of the XYZ system. A number of concerns begin to take shape as the plan emerges. She looks at the current XYZ career site where she finds that someone on her staff has posted several dated and staid-sounding job descriptions for their most frequently filled jobs. Interested applicants are instructed to e-mail a resume or a request for an application blank to one of XYZ's recruiters. Sandra compares this to the careers page of one of their competitors. The competitor's site includes a video walk-through of a typical work area and several testimonials from happy employees.

She also is aware that after a resume is received in their staffing area, her recruiters will route it to the managers who have open positions. Despite having established some basic requirements for many jobs, Sandra worries that these rules are overlooked or inconsistently applied by the managers who receive the resumes.

Sandra also ponders the plight of a colleague who heads up the staffing function at another large company. That company is currently fending off a huge lawsuit related to a claim of gender discrimination in their selection process. If they lose the case, the company will owe back-pay to every female applicant to the company over the past few years – a group of thousands of applicants. Sandra is also aware of government rules that relate to applicants that are received through the Internet and she vows to get on top of this information before implementing XYZ's process.

Sandra realizes that if she designs her recruiting and application site correctly, it can yield more candidates who meet XYZ's qualifications than the current process. It can also help to reduce the risks that her colleague is facing, but only if it is designed correctly …

This chapter focuses on the issue of how to best design recruiting and early stage selection processes within automated staffing systems. While recruiting and selection processes are often distinct, increasing levels of automation has pushed them closer together.

Talent Acquisition: Two Disciplines

Some tension between the recruitment and selection processes is natural. Recruitment requires the organization to reach into the marketplace for possible new employees and entice them to join. Effective selection processes then eliminate most of these hard-earned applicants. As you become involved in the design of recruitment and screening for your organization, it is important to pay attention to the relationship between these processes. When they are working well together, these two processes are coordinated to provide a rich candidate pool and a solid method for identifying those in the pool with the highest potential. The electronic tools that evolved in the marketplace to support each of these processes also vary in their design and outcomes.

Tools to Support Recruitment

The recruitment process in some ways is analogous to deep-sea trawlers that fish by dragging a large net. The recruitment process should reach broadly into a pool of job seekers and then sort through the catch to determine which recruits might meet the organization's hiring criteria. Prior to the mid 1990s, the process relied largely on tactics such as placing employment ads in the right places, establishing strong networks of possible candidates, and collecting resumes for consideration by hiring managers. As the Internet replaced newspaper ads as a primary medium for recruitment, the tools to support this process became more sophisticated. Corporate websites became an HR front-office to job seekers by providing tools for reviewing available openings, expressing interest in specific opportunities, and submitting a resume for consideration. Behind the scenes, information regarding applicants was tracked and sorted by job opening and resumes could be parsed for critical information and then tagged for further consideration in the hiring process. Large resume databases, such as Monster.com, gained popularity as a repository of job seeker information, and recruiting tools were developed to assist recruiters who search through these databases. For example, some search tools crawl through these vast repositories to identify documents with keywords that are similar to the recruiters' criteria. As we will discuss in this chapter, these tools focus on establishing a pool of candidates and mining available information, typically past experience information, from a resume. Resumes alone, however, have limitations when assessing candidate quality because they focus primarily on experience (not knowledge, competencies, or personal characteristics), they do not capture how well the recruit truly performed on each area of experience, and they are not standardized across job seekers.

Tools to Support Screening and Selection

The screening and selection processes have slightly different goals. *Screening* is generally used to remove unqualified job seekers from the staffing process; *selection* tools then focus on choosing the best from the remaining applicants. To extend the trawling analogy, the screening process is similar to a fisherman sorting through his catch, keeping only those fish that meet pre-defined criteria. The screening process in organizations operates in a similar manner. Once a pool of applicants is assembled, critical characteristics are evaluated to determine if each job seeker is qualified for the open position. After the screening phase, the information required of candidates changes. The selection process then focuses on the collection of information that allows the pool of qualified applicants to be narrowed down to those who have the best chance of success on the job. As we will discuss in Chapter 6, selection tools such as tests, structured interviews, and job simulations can be used to assess applicant quality after the screening phase so that the highest-potential candidate can be selected. Automation of both the screening and the selection processes now allows them to be deployed within Internet recruiting and hiring systems. The techniques that are used during the screening process to sort out unqualified candidates as they initially apply for a job will be described in more detail later in this chapter.

Designing Internet Recruiting Sites

A key issue facing HR professionals who are responsible for the design and implementation of recruiting websites is how to best entice job seekers to spend time on the site, exploring information about jobs and the company and ideally applying for one or more opportunities with the company. This issue involves considerations related to corporate image, the company's brand as an employer, and other factors that may affect applicant attitudes. Ultimately, of course, the goal is to entice the job seeker to discover as much as possible about the available opportunities and have the qualified job seekers click on "Apply Now" and commit to becoming an applicant. The next section reviews the most frequently used elements on these websites.

Common Recruiting Site Components

When you are designing a recruiting website, you must balance several different factors. You need to include information that portrays the company in a positive light, capturing the interest and enthusiasm of potential applicants. At the same time, you need to be sure to provide an accurate and realistic view of the company because building expectations that can't be achieved can lead to dissatisfaction and turnover among new employees.[1] You also need to consider what information is critical to obtain from applicants once they have decided to investigate a job opportunity in more detail; however, if your questions are too demanding, personal, or lengthy you risk losing the interest of people you are seeking. As you consider the design of the website components, weigh the pros and cons of each element within the context of your recruiting goals. Also, keep in mind that research in workplace psychology has shown that one of the major determinants of job seeker attitudes toward recruiting websites is the ease with which it can be used, and these attitudes also relate to job seekers' impressions of the company as a whole.[2] Therefore the choices of which components to include should be balanced against the costs of complexity. With these caveats in mind, you should consider website elements in each of the categories that we review below. The box below provides a summary of the frequently used website components.

Common Elements of a Recruiting Website

Website Component	Frequently Used Elements
Employer Overview	Values, mission statement, organization structure, history, typical jobs, benefits, career paths and other opportunities for personal growth, family and work/life accommodations, diversity programs, video testimonials on these topics from current employees
Job Information	Job search by key criteria, job descriptions, basic qualifications and other requirements
Profile Matching	Location, job family, job characteristics, interest and work value profiles; comparison tools between desired and available job aspects
Apply Now	Conditions agreement, personal and contact information collection, applicant communication tools

Employer Overview

At the top level of the recruiting site, material should be presented that describes your organization from an employee perspective. Because this portion of the process is used to convey the unique characteristics of the organization, these pages of the recruiting site have the widest variance across companies. For examples of this, consider the firms in Fortune's list of the 100 best companies to work for. As a group, these organizations tend to focus on their brand as an employer, and the value proposition to their employee populations, more than peer organizations. Some of the larger companies that have frequently appeared on this list provide a good model of how to effectively convey values and culture via a website. Currently, organizations in this category include companies such as Starbucks, Marriott, Cisco Systems, Wegmans Food Markets, and Ernst & Young.[3] Common themes from their sites include a clear statement of the company values and mission statement, descriptions of the primary functions within the company, common job locations, and typical career paths. The emphasis at this stage is on information that applies across the company, but descriptions of highly populated entry-level positions may also be provided if most new employees start their careers with the company within these roles.

Ideally this content is presented in an engaging manner, using quotes and short video or audio clips to describe the company from the point of view of a new employee. An important goal at this stage of the process is to convey a sense of how it feels to the employee to be a part of the company. For example, "innovation" may be an important value for a technology company, so the company description may be written to appeal to new engineering graduates who want to apply cutting-edge technologies in their work.

Several common mistakes should be avoided when constructing this portion of a recruiting site. First, there is a temptation to include overly optimistic views of the company culture. While these statements may sound appealing on the surface, if employees don't recognize them as truthful representations of the culture, they are unlikely to support the view during interactions with job seekers – creating a disconnect between the message and the reality of employees' experience. It is possible that this disconnect could damage both the perceptions of job seekers and the attitudes of current employees who are forced to reconcile the message with the reality of their work experience.

Second, in an effort to appeal to young generations, many employers add features to create atmosphere and interest that provide little value to the job seekers' decision process. These features can be fun and engaging, but if overdone, they can create a barrier to some applicants. Note that there is little research to support the inclusion of music or games to entice job seekers to become job applicants; however, studies have shown a connection between the usability of the site and how attractive the organization appears to job seekers.[4] If these features add complexity to the page and increase the technical requirements of the site, you may run the risk of turning away some job seekers who may not have the patience to wade through the additional features. When advanced features are used that require recently developed software components such as special drivers or browser plug-ins, these features should be placed in the margin of the page and played only at the user's discretion, not as a required portion of the process, otherwise less sophisticated users may experience problems with the site and won't be able to complete the application.

Third, too much information may be presented. Large companies can be difficult to describe in simple, accurate, and attractive terms, but this is the challenge that must be addressed in the design of the top-level page in the recruiting site. Organizations with strong employer overview pages tend to blend the talents of marketing and HR professionals to develop an appealing site.

This portion of the recruiting site, as well as those that follow in the process, should be branded to look and feel like the organization's home page. Typically the marketing function has defined branding standards that specify acceptable colors, design elements, logo placement, and the allowable range of design flexibilities. These standards must be incorporated early in the design process to avoid additional costs of rework if differences are found later. Note that the top-level pages of a career site are often hosted as a portion of the corporate website and maintained by the organization's IT staff. Subsequent stages are frequently hosted by third-party software providers that specialize in recruitment and selection technologies. For most companies it is important that these stages appear seamless to the user, and common branding standards are used to bridge the appearance across these pages. If the appearance is not consistent, candidates can become confused about how the pages of the experience are connected and become frustrated with the navigation. For this reason, flexibility in appearance is often a consideration when choosing a partner for aspects of the online recruiting process.

Job Information

Embedded within the employer information you will want to place an obvious path to a tool that allows the job seeker to search for available jobs. This link is typically placed at several points in the employer overview pages. A common link title is "Search for Jobs." Job seekers who click this link are taken to the next level of the recruiting site, and it is at this point that many organizations use third-party software providers to handle the required features and database transactions. Here again there is some variation among the approaches taken at this step, but many features have now become commonplace for recruiting sites.

The most common features include a multi-criteria search function that allows job seekers to find job listings that match their desired location, job function, and job level. Job listings that match the search criteria are then provided. These listings should also include descriptive information about the job that specifies common responsibilities, a realistic view of the challenges and opportunities provided by the role, and a clear description of the basic qualifications for the role.

A common pitfall when constructing the job information portion of the site is to include available job descriptions for the open positions without consideration of their currency and consistency across jobs. This is problematic because the descriptions are often outdated, written in an inconsistent format, and use varying levels of precision when describing basic job requirements and competencies. As the online system is developed, care should be taken to ensure that the job descriptive information is up to date, in a common format, and consistently flows from the employer overview information that is available in the same website.

Profile Matching

Large organizations can easily have hundreds of open positions at any given time, and job seeker search criteria alone may not provide them with access to the broadest range of roles that could fit their interests. For this reason, many systems also include profile-matching tools that allow the job seeker to enter preferences and interests, and the system returns a list of jobs that may fit. These features extend beyond standard search criteria because they allow the job seeker to create a profile that is more detailed and more personal than the search tools described above will allow. Many systems allow this profile to be saved so that when new jobs are available, the job seeker can quickly evaluate their degree of match to the new opportunities.

To implement a matching function, it is a requirement that the same profile elements be used to describe job seekers and all available positions. These profile elements can contain objective information such as location preferences, desired salary range, and organizational functions of interest, but these elements may also include psychological factors such as work interests, desired work conditions, and work-related values. For example, job seekers may be asked about whether they prefer to work with people or alone, travel frequently or not, and work broadly on many tasks or specialize on fewer. They may also be asked to indicate their desired levels of autonomy, the importance of feedback from their efforts, and the significance of their work beyond their paycheck. Once a profile is entered, the job seeker is presented with a list of jobs along with ratings of how well each job matches the seeker's profile. This type of report allows job seekers to evaluate specific aspects of congruence and misalignment before deciding whether they should complete an application.

Profile-matching functions can have some significant benefits for a recruiting site. They tend to engage the job seeker because the profile is tailored to their personal needs and desires. Additionally, they can provide feedback to the user that can be weighed in their decision-making. Better informed job seekers will be less likely to discontinue a selection process because they learn earlier about features of the role that they find undesirable and may choose not to apply in the first place. Better congruence between the facets of work desired by the job seeker and the reality of the job environment can also lead to higher levels of job satisfaction and tenure in the job.[5] However, it should also be recognized that many job seekers will disregard the degree of match with their preferences and apply for jobs simply because they need one.

The use of profiles for job matching can have some challenges also. The labor required to rate all available jobs in the database on the extent to which various interests and values will be reinforced on the job can be a large undertaking. Typically 10–15 job experts (e.g., supervisors or managers over the positions) are required to generate a reliable profile of the job. Without a reliable profile, the information that is presented back to the candidates could be misleading. An alternative approach offers a profile comparison for just a few jobs, usually those with a high volume of applicants. Under this scenario, only those jobs seekers who are interested in these specific positions can access the profiling questionnaire.

Another common difficultly with job-matching profiles is that recruiters and hiring managers are often temped to obtain the interest and value profiles that were collected from job seekers. This is problematic because the profile data are typically collected purely for the purpose of allowing the job seeker to explore available opportunities in a context of self-insight. As we will discuss in Chapter 11, the subsequent use of these data for purposes other than those described to the job seeker is in violation of data privacy regulations. As a best practice, when profile data are obtained from job seekers, the information is not preserved and is unavailable to decision-makers. Thus the purpose for matching tools is focused on enlightened job search not on candidate selection; the value is in the fact that some job seekers decide not to apply for ill-fitting opportunities while others may see opportunities where they may not have seen them before.

Apply Now

Once job seekers have identified one or more open positions of interest, the next step is to submit an application or a similar statement of their interest. This is often managed by a web page that is available under a link titled "Submit an Application" or "Apply Now." It is during this step that the job seeker may transition to a more formal status of "applicant," a status that has both practical and legal implications.

Once the job seeker has indicated interest in submitting an application, he or she will often be presented with a page that requests their agreement to the terms and conditions of the process. When designing the agreement step, consider including clauses that relate to the honesty of the user's responses as well as the security of the process. Statements should also be included that ask the job seeker to acknowledge how their data will be used (more information about this topic is provided in Chapter 11). Examples of these conditions are outlined in the box below. Of course, regardless of their agreement, there is no guarantee that job seekers won't exaggerate when completing the process.

Example:
Job Candidate Agreement Points

Job Candidates should agree …

- that the information they provide will be accurate. This condition encourages honesty in response and is often paired with a statement regarding the consequences of inaccurate application information (typically immediate dismissal).
- that they acknowledge how the information to be collected will be used by the company. This condition is important for defining the allowable purposes and security restrictions on the data provided by the applicant. This issue will be elaborated in Chapter 11.
- that they will not copy or share the information that is included in the process with others. This point is critical when the screening and selection process includes assessment material that is designed under the assumption that applicants do not receive copies of the material and preferred responses in advance. We will return to this issue in Chapter 9.

If the job seeker agrees to the stated conditions, they are allowed to progress to the next phase of the application; if they decline, they should be excluded from the selection process. Next, the process will request personal information from the job seeker, including contact information for further steps. Some systems allow job seekers to prepare draft or anonymous applications, so that the information can be considered carefully before it is officially submitted. Another useful feature that many employers include is a communications area that allows the job seeker and the recruiter to leave messages for one another directly in a private area of the recruiting site, thereby keeping all communications within the recruiting system. This feature is an advantage to job seekers who are currently employed and wish to keep their job search private and to recruiters who need to maintain a record of their interactions with many candidates.

The online application itself will often contain questions that allow the organization to screen and select the applicants that are the most qualified. Common methods used in the screening process are the focus of the next section.

The Apply Now step is a turning point in the process. The job seeker may not be an official applicant yet, but he or she will satisfy several conditions of the legal definition by clicking the Apply Now button. Once the online application is complete and submitted, for most purposes the job seeker should now be considered to be an applicant. (The technical definition of an applicant will be discussed later in this chapter.) Also, the intent of the process shifts once the online application is complete. Up to this point, the purpose of the recruiting process has been to entice as many qualified job seekers as possible to submit an application; after the application step is initiated, the organization's goal should shift toward those applicants who are qualified for the role and are predicted to have the highest potential for success on the job.

Designing Online Screening Tools

The connection between the recruitment and screening processes is critical; the larger the pool of applicants, the more likely it will be that well-qualified candidates will emerge, but the screening tools must be strong enough to identify them from the crowd. There are two approaches that are commonly used for the initial screening of applicants when automated systems are being used: some systems rely heavily on the information contained on a resume, others require applicants to complete structured questions that can be weighted and scored. Many companies also use a combination of these two approaches. Other options are possible also; for example, some companies give tests to all applicants as a screening method. We focus here on the two methods that are usually deployed in automated systems.[6]

Resume-Centric Applicant Screening

Inflow of applicants via the Internet creates an issue: potentially far too many interested job seekers may be collected from which to assemble an applicant pool. Finding qualified candidates in a database of thousands can then become a needle-in-a-haystack problem.

Resume storage tools are typically built to work within an applicant tracking system. They allow for storage and retrieval of individual resumes based on a text search of the information contained within the document. These resume-centric tools operate from the assumption that the resume is an accurate and essential description of the job seeker, and they tend to appeal to recruiters who have long operated with a received resume as a spark for subsequent recruiting events.

Parsing tools are often included in systems that operate based on a resume. These tools will deconstruct the resume, and put relevant information in a database, thereby eliminating the need for manual entry of the information. For example, common information such as name, address, educational degrees and institutions, and certifications will be identified and captured within the system. Despite this automated convenience, these tools are not highly accurate, and it is recommended that HR staff review the material that is drawn from a resume in this manner to avoid the proliferation of errors generated when a phrase on a resume is misclassified by the system.

Parsing and keyword-search tools tend to rely on technology advancements in the attempt to reduce the many issues that arise when resumes are used as a starting point for recruitment. These new features include internal logic rules that are designed to avoid issues of mismatched terms or overlooked work history descriptions that can occur when, for example, detecting meaning from the context of the statement that includes the word "Java," and correctly parsing the term as a computer language instead of an island in Indonesia.

The many challenges for these resume-centric tools stem from the fact that these tools base their value on the efficient management of the information that can be consistently found on a resume. Of course, the use of resumes as an indicator of candidate quality has many severe limitations. Resumes cannot truly measure competencies, skills, abilities, or other job-relevant characteristics. While the resume can tell you various biographical facts (education, jobs held, certifications, etc.), they do not index the quality of prior work nor the learning gained from prior experience. These essential characteristics can best be determined via more advanced assessment and interviewing techniques.

The value of resume parsing and search tools is in their ability to create a pool of job seekers that can be considered further by the employer from a much larger database of resumes. Even this purpose has serious drawbacks because job seekers may not use terms or phrases that correspond to the searched aspects of the job, so well-qualified job seekers may go unnoticed while less qualified candidates who used more descriptive phasing in their resumes may be detected by a word-search technique.

Despite these shortcomings, many staffing systems remain resume-centric: recruiters request them, candidates provide them, and therefore software providers have developed tools to support the use of the resume as a central component of the staffing process. Organizations that seek to identify high-quality employees will focus on tools that are better able to achieve higher levels of insight, leaving the resume to be used only as a description of the applicant's background and experience to provide context to interviewers and hiring managers.

Questionnaire-Based Applicant Screening

To fill the shortcomings of resume storage and parsing tools, many career websites, and the automated systems that underlie them, present structured questions that are designed to provide standardized inputs for the selection of candidates. These tools provide a means to construct and/or choose questions for administration to job seekers and may include tools to score the items. These features can then group or order candidates according to their standing on the factors that are assessed. In their simplest form these tools may be viewed as online resume builders, asking questions that allow job seekers to respond to questions that are carefully constructed and validated.

Applicant screening tools of this variety are designed to efficiently capture information that is necessary for conducting a rough sorting of the applicants. The purpose at this phase is to eliminate those who are clearly unqualified and, when these tools are designed and implemented effectively, provide a standardized method for categorizing job seekers according to their suitability as applicants for specific positions.

Screening systems can offer a range of options for collecting job-relevant information about job seekers. Common question content for applicant screening includes work and educational history (some systems may extract this information from a resume and have candidates review the extraction for accuracy and currency instead of requiring the time from your HR staff); basic qualification requirements (such as licenses, certifications, years of experience in specific roles); and broader questions about applicant background (for example, questions about experience with specific equipment, work processes, or business issues). In each case, these questions should be carefully developed to have clear relationships to the job for which they are used. More examples of questions that are used to assess basic qualifications are shown in the box below.

> **Example:**
> **Common Online Screening Questions**
>
> Are you legally authorized to work in the United States on a full-time, continuing basis?
> ☐ Yes ☐ No
>
> Will you now or in the future require sponsorship for employment visa status?
> ☐ Yes ☐ No
>
> Do you currently hold a valid U.S. driver's license?
> ☐ Yes ☐ No
>
> Has your driver's license been suspended or revoked in the past 3 years?
> ☐ Yes ☐ No
>
> Indicate your highest level of education:
> [Select education level ▼]
>
> Indicate any relevant professional licenses or certifications:
> [Select job-related licenses and certifications ▼]
>
> Are you willing to relocate?
> ☐ Yes ☐ No
> Where are you willing to relocate to?
> [Select job locations ▼]
>
> How many years of sales experience do you have?
> ☐ None ☐ Less than 1 year ☐ 1–3 years ☐ More than 3 years
>
> Are you willing to work in a position in which your compensation will be based partly on commission or incentive pay?
> ☐ Yes ☐ No

Common Risks Associated with Online Screening

Sophisticated versions of these screening tools are based on the same measurement principles as we discussed in Chapter 3, especially where scores are set based on the value of a particular response for predicting job success. However, unlike professionally developed tests, the design of the scoring scheme in many automated screening tools may be delegated to individual system users. For example, some screening tools allow users to define custom screening questions, assign weights and scores to each question, and calculate a total score. These features should be considered with extreme caution. Although software developers and some system users may view these flexibilities as a benefit, they can carry some substantial risks. When question construction, weighting, and scoring features are available for user configuration, the responsibility for ensuring effectiveness, fairness, job relatedness, and consistency of their application can be too easily overlooked. Well-designed systems will allow for central controls to enable, for example, screening criteria to be determined and applied consistently across similar positions in an organization by measurement experts who can ensure that proper procedures are followed to validate the requirements. Decisions regarding how to set basic qualifications and other early screening criteria can lead to serious issues if they are based on factors that are too strict or bear little relationship to actual performance of the job; therefore designers and implementers of these tools should enquire about the how the process will be validated. Frequently, the job requirements that are used for screening questions are based on content validation processes that use a carefully designed process to collect subject matter expert judgments of their appropriateness.[7]

Another challenge with these measures is that the degree of insight that can be obtained with screening questionnaires alone tends to be limited. These tools are typically used very early in a selection process, before many job seekers feel committed to the process. Therefore screening tools should be kept brief, so that candidates are not overburdened early in the process. Processes that include long screening questionnaires run the risk that qualified candidates will abandon their applications.

Additionally, because screening information is collected early in the hiring process, wide access to this step is desirable and this part of the process is usually placed on public access websites (i.e., no passwords are required). But public access also limits the type of questions that should be used. Because the employer does not have control over who is completing the questions, questions that measure ability, knowledge, and skill that have clear right-and-wrong answers should usually be avoided because they are more likely to be susceptible to collaboration and other forms of cheating. Ideally, the screening questions used at this stage focus on biographical information and experience summaries that can be verified later in the process (e.g., during interviews and reference checks), so that applicants will be less likely to benefit from the assistance of others. Also, screening systems should avoid tools that focus heavily on the measurement of personality, because some forms of these tests use questions that may be perceived as too personal or invasive for candidates that may be just beginning to explore an employment relationship with the organization. Once past the screening phase, these stronger measures that provide deeper levels of insight can be deployed in the form of securely administered tests; a topic we review in the next chapter.

Defining Basic Qualifications

A final area of caution regarding automated screening measures concerns their use for the assessment of basic qualifications. When designed appropriately, screening questions can quickly identify those job seekers who lack fundamental job requirements so that they may be excluded from the applicant pool without further consideration. This is useful for employers in the United States because there are strict rules for maintaining records on qualified applicants, a topic that we will review in more detail in the next section. The benefit for employers is that basic qualifications can be used to exclude unqualified job seekers from their applicant pools; only the records for qualified applicants need then be maintained.

The most precise standard for defining a basic qualification has been set by the U.S. Office of Federal Contracts Compliance Programs (OFCCP). This branch of the U.S. Department of Labor has responsibility for ensuring that any employer who holds contracts with the U.S. Government exceeding $50,000 a year complies with a variety of employment and contracting rules. According to the OFCCP's rules, a basic qualification that is used for excluding a job seeker from an applicant pool must meet three criteria.[8] First, the qualification must not involve a comparison between applicants. For example, a qualification of two years of sales experience is non-comparative, but if the employer was interested in the *most* experienced sales persons within a pool of job seekers, this would be a comparative qualification because the job seekers must be compared to one another to find those who qualify. Second, the qualification must be objective (i.e., not dependent upon judgment). For example, the qualification cannot state that the job seeker's past experience be at a "good company with a solid reputation" since this would require a judgment about the quality of the company. "Experience in the retail industry" would be a more objective criterion. Third, the qualification must be relevant to performance of the particular position and enable the employer to accomplish its business-related goals.

In order to use basic qualifications to exclude unqualified job seekers from an applicant pool, the OFCCP further indicted that the qualifications must be either advertised (e.g., posted on a website) or established prior to considering any job seeker for a particular position (such as when searching an external resume database). Ideally, when you are considering the design of your online screening process, you carefully consider the basic qualifications that are included so they match the federal guidelines. Screening questions can then be defined and constructed within your online screening process to quickly sort job seekers to identify those who qualify as applicants.

Critical Issues to Resolve

Several issues must be addressed as online recruiting and screening systems are designed and implemented. These issues include: (a) determining the point in the process when a job seeker becomes an official applicant, (b) deciding on the depth of the assessment to be used in the process, and (c) planning for how applicants will progress through the process. These issues are reviewed briefly below.

When is a Job Seeker an Applicant?

The point where a job seeker becomes an applicant is important. This is especially true in the United States because U.S. employers are required to keep extensive records about their applicants. Ideally, many job seekers are obtained in the recruiting process, but only the truly qualified job seekers actually become job applicants. The employer thus reduces the burden of keeping records on job seekers who are not qualified. Should a legal issue develop related to the process, having fewer qualified applicants can also reduce employer liability. Here again, the rules determined by the OFCCP serve as an important guidepost for understanding this process in the context of Internet-based selection processes. According to the OFCCP, an individual is considered an "Internet Applicant" when four criteria are met:

1. the individual submits an "expression of interest" in employment through the Internet (for example, by submitting a profile for an open position);
2. the company considers the individual for employment in a particular position;
3. the individual's expression of interest indicates that the individual possesses the basic qualifications for the position (per the definition of basic qualifications described above); and
4. the individual at no point in the selection process, prior to receiving an offer of employment, removes him or herself from further consideration or otherwise indicates that he or she is no longer interested in the position.

Designers of online selection processes should map their selection stages to the criteria defined above to ensure that the applicant pools are precisely defined.

Another way to reduce unqualified job seekers is to provide them with ample information about the position before they are given a chance to express interest via the online application. A clearly defined procedure should be in place to allow applicants to take themselves out of the process if they are no longer interested in the position after viewing job information and the qualification requirements. By following these procedures, you will reduce the pool of job seekers to only those who are both interested and qualified in your jobs.

How Detailed Should the Screening Process be?

When designing screening processes, be careful to match the level of detail in the measurement with the size of your selection requirement. For example, if for a particular position you hire three people a year from a process that begins with thirty resumes, an investment in online screening tools will be unlikely to pay off. Instead, the use of online resume submission processes will probably be sufficient to fill the need. On the other hand, if you hire three hundred people for a process that attracts three thousand resumes a year, you will likely benefit from the structure and accuracy of an automated screening tool. Many large organizations receive applicant volumes that can exceed hundreds of thousands of applicants in a year. In these situations the automation of the application and screening process is essential for managing the workflow, ensuring consistency, and quickly identifying the applicants with the highest potential for success on the job.

How Should Applicants be Progressed through the Selection Process?

Computer-based tools also offer some new options for how decisions are made about job applicants. As information is collected in the early phases of the screening process, decisions about who becomes an applicant, and which applicants are allowed into later phases of assessment, can be scripted into the tools. Automated scoring and sorting of applicants can be both a convenience and a risk. When you have thousands of applicants in your staffing process, it is important to prioritize the applicants so that recruiters can focus on those who will have the highest chance of succeeding on the job, say the top 20% of a large pool of applicants. Well-designed scoring rules can batch the applicants, first by eliminating from further consideration those who don't meet basic qualifications, and then by grouping the remaining applicants based on their standing on the questions that have been shown to have a strong relationship to performance on the job.

But, as we noted above, be aware that these scoring tools should be used cautiously. The development of scores and passing rules should be guided by an expert in measurement of this type to ensure that only qualified applicants are getting through. Automated scoring routines can eliminate qualified candidates if they are not properly calibrated.

Communication with candidates regarding their progression through the system should also be closely managed. Although many systems are capable of immediately rejecting candidates who don't meet pre-defined standards, this should be avoided because candidates will understand that the computer triggered the decision without human input. This may inspire some candidates to submit false profiles to figure out which profiles will be admitted to the next phase of the process. Alternatively, a delay (often just a day or two) can be programmed between the submission of a profile and the generation of a rejection notice to unqualified job seekers. Furthermore, applicants who meet the basic qualifications but are not sorted into the group slated for urgent follow-up action should be held for a longer period of time in case the top group gets depleted as the selection process continues.

Moving candidates that succeed in the process quickly into the selection step is important so that they remain engaged in the process. Automated systems can often generate an invitation to the next set of assessments, including an embedded link and log-in information to a testing or other assessment event. Here again, some delay (often no more than a day) can often be preferable to immediately transferring candidates into the next step. Rapid transfer into the next phase can appear to force candidates into a testing event that they are not immediately prepared for, leaving some candidates at a disadvantage.

Summary

In this chapter we have reviewed the fundamental concepts and techniques that are used as job seekers are introduced to the company and the job opportunities it offers. Techniques for collecting initial information from job seekers, checking their qualifications, and identifing those with high potential were also summarized. These tools are usually not designed with the intent of providing enough information to make a hiring decision, however. In Chapter 6 we will examine the next step in the process, where additional insight about top candidates is generated by administering tests and other online measurement tools. Key design tips from this chapter are summarized in the box overleaf.

Tips:
The Design of Online Recruiting and Screening Systems

- Understand how the recruitment and screening processes operate in your organization. Design online tools to create a seamless flow between these functions.
- Create an organization description that is informative, realistic, engaging, and short. Use web technologies that create interest and appeal without raising the technical requirements for the site beyond common standards.
- Include features that allow job seekers to explore multiple job openings before they pick those of high interest.
- When many jobs are available, include profiling tools that match self-reports of job seeker interests, values, and skills with the characteristics of available jobs.
- Prepare job descriptions that are up to date and realistic. Include both selling points and challenges for the roles.
- Require job seekers to agree to conditions that ensure the accuracy and security of the content of your online recruiting process.
- Carefully construct screening questions to match requirements for basic qualifications (especially if your application is to be used in the United States).
- Deploy additional screening questions that allow you to sort applicants into groups that correspond to their likelihood of success on the job. Verify the predictive capability of these questions through validation research.

Chapter 6

Deploying Automated Tests

Choosing the right assessment tool and implementing it properly is crucial to the success of your staffing program. Just as a golfer must select the right club and execute the proper swing to hit the ball as near as possible to the pin, your challenge is to choose the right type of assessment tool and deploy it properly in your online staffing system to ensure that you are able to identify talent that hits the performance mark. A wide range of assessment tools is available from which to choose. This chapter provides guidance on essential topics for planning and implementing online assessments, including:

- types of assessment tools that are available;
- important considerations for using different types of assessments;
- key technology considerations for online assessment;
- critical issues to be resolved in planning for the use of online assessments.

Types of Assessment Tools

In the HR world, the focus of assessment is upon knowledge, skills, abilities, and other personal characteristics (KSAOs) that are required to successfully perform job tasks and demonstrate required competencies. Accordingly, different types of assessment instruments are available to measure certain KSAOs and focus on different content areas, depending upon the purpose of the assessment. Alternative assessment formats may be used to elicit and capture candidate responses, posing trade-offs in cost efficiency, predictive effectiveness, and fidelity to the job.

Good to Know:
Terminology

- *Job knowledge:* Information needed to perform the work required on the job
- *Skill:* Level of proficiency on a specific task or group of tasks
- *Ability:* A defined domain of cognitive, perceptual, psychomotor, or physical functioning
- *Personal characteristic:* A trait, attitude or disposition that describes individuals
- *Competencies:* Related behaviors that demonstrate job proficiency, which may require any combination of enabling KSAOs

Assessment Content – More Than Meets the Eye

The KSAOs measured by assessments can be pictured as an iceberg (Figure 6.1). Above the surface you see behavior and outcomes manifested as competencies, skills, and knowledge. Below the surface are a larger and broader set of underlying capabilities and attributes that you do not see. These are the abilities, traits, attitudes, motivation, and interests that enable learning, development, and application of knowledge, skills, and competencies in a wide range of situations and contexts.

Above the surface – measuring proficiency. Knowledge and skill assessments are useful in gauging the current state of a candidate's proficiency in a subject matter or set of tasks. Examples of job-specific knowledge and skills include: knowing whether a contract complies with real estate laws, identifying the correct dosage of a drug for a patient, calculating the five-year depreciation of plant equipment, or typing forty-five words per minute. Depending upon the nature and complexity of the job, knowledge and skills may be learned during initial on-the-job training, or may be prerequisites and, thus, important to assess before hire. For example, customer service representatives may receive initial on-the-job training in explaining new products and handling customer complaints, but they may be

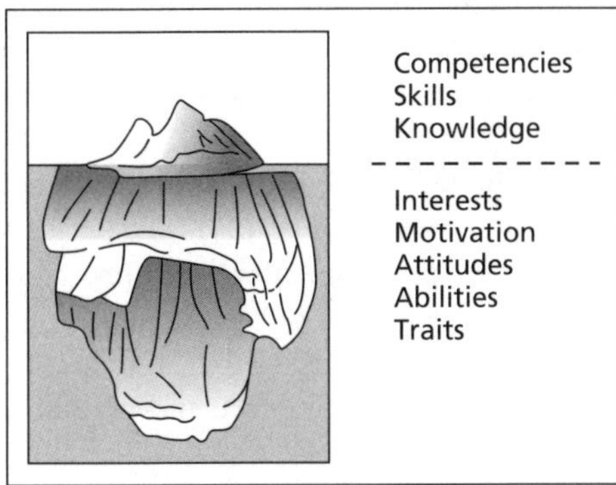

Figure 6.1 The Iceberg Model of human characteristics

required to already possess basic skills in communication and operating a computer keyboard.

Below the surface – measuring potential. Assessments of abilities, personality traits, attitudes, and other personal characteristics are useful to measure a candidate's future potential (aptitude) in such critical areas as learning and development, relationship building, and adapting to change. It is difficult to know by talking to candidates or reviewing their resumes whether they will be successful in these areas in the future. Fortunately, you can assess candidate potential using professionally developed instruments that are based on psychological measurement principles (outlined in Chapter 3).

Abilities and personal characteristics are both general and enduring. They are general in that they enable the performance of a wide range of tasks in different contexts, and underlie the development of various competencies. For example, the ability to use deductive reasoning[1] enables development of specific job skills as diverse as correctly applying rules for approving health insurance claims, or troubleshooting the causes of an IT system error. Abilities and personal characteristics are enduring, in that they are a combination of inherited potential and long-term development that takes place during the formative years of human development. Once developed, they do not quickly change, and thus are not amenable to training in the short term. Case in point: a truly extroverted (outgoing, socially bold) person at age twenty is likely to be extroverted at age thirty, barring any personal catastrophic events. Pre-hire assessments of abilities and personality attributes are common in talent acquisition programs.

Some assessments focus on biographical information (biodata), which may draw from a wide range of life experience questions. Biodata instruments are sometimes developed expressly to predict job performance, and not designed to measure (i.e., yield scores for) KSAOs that underlie performance. Other biodata tools may be designed to measure KSAOs that underlie and predict performance, similar to ability and trait measures.

Assessment Format – Something Old, Something New

Although it may seem surprising in light of technology advances, the multiple-choice format continues to be widely used in assessment instruments, including those delivered online. Computer technology offers much potential for interactive multimedia assessments that simulate jobs and which may incorporate a wide range of formats for delivering scenarios and capturing and scoring responses (see Chapter 12). However, when it comes to cost-effective development and administration, reliable scoring, and predictive effectiveness, multiple-choice questions are difficult to beat, particularly for knowledge and aptitude assessments. This format is quite amenable to online delivery and scoring, although care should be taken when designing assessments for online delivery (see Part III of this book).

Simulations are becoming increasingly popular, as technology has increased the feasibility of alternative presentation formats. A wide continuum of options exists for online simulation delivery and the capture of candidate responses, ranging from "low fidelity" written or video scenarios with multiple-choice response options, to "high fidelity" multimedia job simulations that require more complex candidate responses; some even provide automated scoring. Because of the higher costs of development, time requirements for administration, and complexity of scoring, online simulations are less frequently used at this time (see Chapter 12 for further discussion of the future of online assessment).

Online systems may also play a role in structured interviews. Automated generation of interview forms and rating guides, and computer-aided scoring are now available, providing an effective means of standardizing and organizing information that is generated via traditional face-to-face interviews.

Summary of Assessment Types

Assessment of qualifications:

- Application pre-screen: questions about willingness to accept work conditions and meeting basic employment requirements.
- Training and experience: inventory of job qualifications, training, experience, and/or education.

Uses: identify candidates who meet qualifications and are willing to comply with requirements.
Advantages: checklist format offers low cost and minimal time requirements.
Considerations: legal requirements for applicant tracking (see Chapters 3 and 5).

Assessment of proficiency/competency:

- Knowledge test: measures subject matter expertise and mastery.
- Skill test: measures capability to perform a task or demonstrate a technique (mental, psychomotor, or physical).

Uses: employee selection, promotion, placement, development, and training.
Advantages: multiple-choice tests are cost- and time-efficient, objective and reliable; selecting employees with knowledge/skill proficiency saves training time and expenses.
Considerations: Helpful to ensure minimal competency, but may not discern top talent.

Assessment of potential:

- Cognitive ability test: measures mental capabilities such as verbal, reasoning, numerical, spatial, and perceptual abilities.
- Personality test: self-report inventory measuring traits such as conscientiousness, agreeableness, extraversion, stability, and openness to experience (the "Big-Five" personality traits).
- Attitude test: self-report inventory measuring behavioral intentions, demonstrated by beliefs, opinions, self-descriptions, and endorsements of behavior (may also measure Big-Five traits).
- Motivation and interest inventory: self-report survey of likes and dislikes, preferences, and interests.
- Biodata questionnaire: self-report measure of life experiences, which correlate with job performance.

Continued

Summary of Assessment Types (Continued)

- Situational judgment test: measures various content areas and competencies by analyzing a written scenario (or video) and selecting the best course of action.

Uses: forecast future job success for employee selection, promotion, placement, development, succession planning.
Advantages: multiple-choice tests are cost- and time-efficient, objective and reliable; ROI from improved employment decisions.
Considerations: cognitive ability tests are generally the best predictors of job performance, but some demographic groups tend to score lower on them; thus, local validation studies are recommended to defend their use, when feasible. Personality and attitude tests tend to have small differences between demographic groups and predict different aspects of job performance than cognitive tests, so the combined use of cognitive and non-cognitive tests can be powerful. Biodata forms can be effective predictors of performance but may not generalize across situations and tend to have a short shelf life. Situational Judgment tests appear job-related to candidates and may complement cognitive and non-cognitive tests, but tend to take longer to administer and may also result in score differences among demographic groups.

Behavioral assessment methods:

- Job simulation: scenario-based test or staged exercise, often with role players and evaluators who assess candidate behavior in a "live" setting that simulates the job (these may also incorporate online multimedia technology in their delivery).
- Structured interview: scripted oral questions with standard evaluation criteria to measure various content areas and competencies (typically those not amenable to written assessment; such as communication and interpersonal skills).

Uses: assess proficiency or forecast success potential for employee selection, promotion, placement, development, succession planning.
Advantages: measure capabilities and qualities that cannot be assessed via written exams; high fidelity of test format increases candidate acceptance.
Considerations: increased time and cost to develop, and to administer and score by trained interviewers or evaluators; high fidelity to specific job tasks decreases the degree to which performance may generalize.

Considerations for Using Different Types of Assessments

There are number of key factors that you should consider when planning your assessment program, including: the purpose of the assessment, size of the program, job type and level, validation requirements, legal defensibility, and the availability of resources to support the development and implementation of the assessment system.

Purpose of Assessment

Knowledge/skill tests are useful to assess candidates when the job requires immediate proficiency in certain subject matter or task performance. Aptitude and personality tests are useful to assess candidates when you want to know their potential to learn and perform successfully in a wide range of situations. Simulations are useful when you want to see if candidates can perform specific behaviors.

Tips

Use ...	*When ...*
Knowledge/skill tests	The job requires proficiency in certain critical areas, you wish to avoid the cost of training, and you cannot rely on self-reported knowledge/skill.
Cognitive ability tests	The job requires significant learning, problem solving, or analysis of new information in a wide range of situations.
Personality or attitude tests	The job requires significant interaction with people, or if work habits and turnover are a special concern.
Simulations and assessment centers	It is important to observe the candidate's behavior under realistic conditions before they are hired, and when simulation delivery and scoring are feasible.

Program Size

The volume of candidate testing will dictate, or at least constrain, the types of assessments that are feasible. Large high-volume staffing programs require optimum efficiency in assessment delivery, scoring, and the application of decision criteria to accommodate the need for high capacity and speed in processing candidates. To this end, brief (e.g., 30–40 minute) objectively scored multiple-choice test batteries measuring a range of abilities and attributes may be deployed and scored online to select high-potential candidates from thousands of applicants. Because of the increased exposure of large-volume programs, it is important to have a large bank of assessment content that can be rotated to protect the security and integrity of the assessment system (because applicants may share information).

Job Type and Level

As a rule of thumb, the higher the job level, the more in-depth the assessment will be, and the less likely that the information will be used for purely mechanical decision-making. Two factors drive this trend: practical constraints and the impact of the job on the organization. For example, candidates for hourly non-exempt jobs are commonly assessed with tests of basic skills and attributes. Because most high-volume staffing programs are focused on these types of jobs, selection testing is typically brief and used to make large-scale mechanical (quantitative) filtering decisions in order to keep time and costs to a minimum. On the other hand, professional and managerial jobs are fewer in number and have a higher impact upon the organization. As a result, candidates for these jobs are typically assessed with more in-depth tests of analytical abilities and personality traits; job simulations and assessment centers that combine multiple measures are also used frequently for jobs at higher levels in the organization. The resulting assessment information is often used to support not only selection decision-making, but also to provide narrative (qualitative) information for developmental feedback to candidates, or to enable HR managers to size up "bench strength" and identify future leaders for succession planning in the organization. Figure 6.2 illustrates the typical job level-assessment length relationship (the wide bars summarize typical assessment time; the narrow lines extend to show times for more in-depth assessments).

Validation Requirements

To ensure that your testing program will be effective in identifying candidates who possess the talent needed to be successful on the job, your plan should include verification that the assessment tools are valid for your intended use of the scores they produce. (In Chapter 3, we outlined fundamental measurement concepts, including test validation.) If your talent acquisition program includes proficiency (knowledge/skill) assessments, validation may be accomplished with modest resources within several weeks under a content-based strategy. If your assessment program includes aptitude tests (cognitive

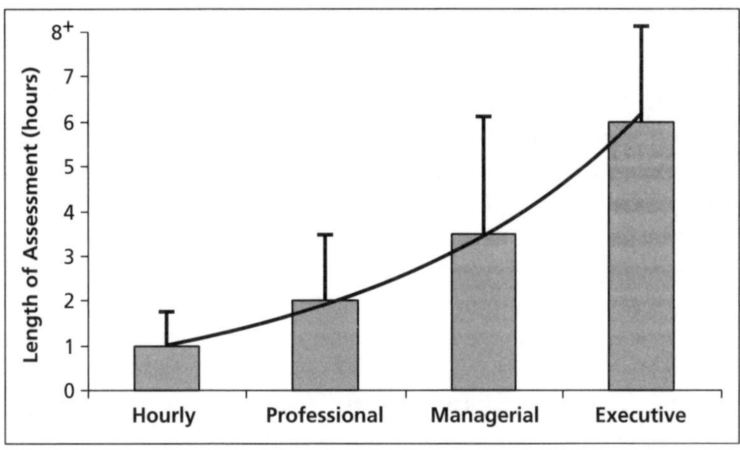

Figure 6.2 Length of assessment as a function of job level

ability, personality, attitude, motivation, biodata), substantially more time and resources may be required in order to complete a criterion-related study (several months and potentially hundreds of participants). However, when pre-existing validation data are available, an efficient method can be used to transport test validity evidence from one setting to another for similar jobs, comparable in time and effort to a content validation study. To be legally defensible in the United States, the validation data and transport study must meet certain requirements outlined in the *Uniform Guidelines.*[2]

Legal Defensibility

An added benefit to confirming that the assessment tools you choose are valid is that you will be armed to defend their use in the event of a legal challenge to your program. (In Chapter 3 and the Appendix, we outlined key legal considerations in employment testing.) Some important considerations in planning your testing program from a legal standpoint are as follows:

- You should be prepared to defend your choice of assessment tools; that is, how they relate to requirements of the job, and what alternatives you considered, including different tests, scoring methods and the minimum passing score. The *Uniform Guidelines*[3] require employers to investigate alternative selection procedures and methods for using them when conducting a validation study. When alternative procedures are available that provide comparable validity, employers are expected to use the procedure or combination that produces smaller differences in pass rates among demographic groups.

- To ensure demographic diversity, you should examine test norms and historical data to understand the impact on passing rates that your program is likely to have for different demographic groups. A pilot test administration will be helpful to evaluate the local impact of the assessment. Tests may manifest differences in average scores or passing rates among demographic groups (e.g., gender, race/ethnicity). This is particularly true for cognitive tests of knowledge, skill or ability.
- Once the program is implemented, plan on periodically monitoring candidate test performance and passing rates to ensure that the assessment is operating as intended with respect to candidate flow and pass rates. In the United States, be prepared to respond to federal government agency inquiries and potential audits.[4]

Resource Planning

Few organizations employ internal staff with the psychometric expertise needed to design, develop, and maintain assessment instruments. Therefore, it is likely that you will need to consult with a workplace psychologist regarding the design of appropriate tools, or the choice of tools from an assessment vendor (who may also offer consulting services). The consultant will need to work closely with your technology group and any HRIS vendors to ensure that delivery systems are available, configured properly and well supported. The consultant should also ensure that information is captured and distributed in an efficient and secure manner and that the systems are integrated correctly.

Technology Considerations for Online Assessment

When designed properly, technology should be virtually transparent in online assessment. By this, we mean that the assessment should measure the intended KSAO – nothing more and nothing less. The aim of online assessment is to avoid the influence of extraneous factors such as computer knowledge and skills, Internet connection speed, and computer screen resolution. We want to obtain a pure and standardized measure of aptitude or proficiency. To this end, there are a number of design considerations that you should heed, whether building your own or adopting a vendor's online assessment tools. Key considerations are outlined below; additional considerations for assessment systems are outlined in Chapter 8.

Presentation of Item Content

Test questions should be presented completely on the computer monitor display in a clearly legible font that is consistent with typical printed sizes, without the need for scrolling or selecting from drop-down menus to see the entire question. Avoid the use of fonts, colors, or other features that might affect the difficulty of the KSAO measured (e.g., in a test of accuracy in processing business forms that are typically printed in Times Roman 12-point font, the test might be made too easy if rendered on the computer display in Arial 20 point font, as a programmer might be tempted to do to fill up the screen). If an alternative paper-and-pencil test form is used, the online version should mirror the look-and-feel of the paper form to provide a comparable test-taking experience and to enable the use of mixed delivery modes. The software should be designed to enable immediate displays without delays due to connectivity (i.e., Internet speed or traffic), and should function comparably under different display resolution settings.

Navigation Features and Functions

Online assessments should enable examinees to answer questions and advance with minimum effort – the fewer clicks on the mouse needed to advance, the better! Navigation through the test should be simple, using easily accessible click-points (e.g., radio buttons, check boxes, text/image blocks, or drag-and-drop) for easy response, with the capability to change or remove answers, and to skip and later review items. It is important that status information be displayed during the assessment informing examinees of their progress (e.g., items answered, items remaining, time remaining). Ideally, assessments should be presented using the full computer display (known as "kiosk mode") with browser and operating system functions disabled to avoid unintentional disruption or intentional tampering with the testing session.

Examinee Instructions

Candidates should be provided an opportunity to become familiar with the test delivery interface to ensure that they understand how to navigate and respond to questions. To this end, a general tutorial should be provided in advance of the assessment, including an overview of navigation features and functions, status information, and a practice test session. It is also advisable to include an automated software diagnostic tool that checks to make sure that the candidate's computer is configured properly to run the assessment software. The diagnostic tool will usually check such items as the pop-up blocker settings, the Internet browser version, and for any special software requirements, such as JavaScript or ActiveX.

Testing Time

Online assessments should be designed to ensure that response and navigation time is reasonable within the test time limit. It is important to ensure that the nature of assessment is not altered by time delays or variations created by the software interface. For timed tests, particularly those with highly restrictive time limits, it is also important to ensure that the timer is accurate under a range of conditions. Local computer clocks are not always reliable; therefore the assessment system should provide an independent timing mechanism for the test.

Security

Maintaining the security of online assessment instruments is central to preserving their integrity and shelf life. Important security features that should be built into the test administration software include: authorized credentials (ID and password) required to access the assessments; time-limited key-based test administration (each administration requires a unique code to launch, and must be started within a limited time period); disabled browser functions (e.g., copy, cut, paste, print); encrypted data transmission (e.g., Secure Socket Layer; Secure HTTP); and secure protocols for handling broken sessions (system down or lost Internet connection). Additional system security considerations are discussed in Chapters 9 and 11, and future trends in online assessment delivery that may contribute to security are outlined in Chapter 12.

Critical Issues to Resolve

As you have seen, a variety of assessment tools are available to serve a range of talent acquisition needs. Key considerations were outlined for designing online assessments, which, if attended to, will greatly enhance the effectiveness of your staffing program. As you move forward in planning your program, you can begin to map out your strategy by working with experts and addressing the following key issues:

- *What KSAOs should be measured?* Conduct a job analysis to identify important job tasks and competencies, and required KSAOs to assess before hire. Create a blueprint specifying what the assessments should measure.
- *What types of assessments will meet your organizational needs in a cost-effective manner?* Identify assessment tools that measure the target KSAOs within any constraints that you have for testing time, cost, and resource requirements for implementation.
- *Determine whether to buy or build.* Some key considerations in weighing the pros and cons are:
  - R&D time and costs for the assessment tool and delivery software vs. an off-the-shelf (OTS) solution: Depending upon the scope of the assessment system, the investment to build can easily run in the hundreds of thousands of dollars and take months or years. An OTS solution will be faster and cheaper in the near term (e.g., in the first few years of operation).
  - Costs for hardware, software operating system, maintenance and upgrades, and technical support staff vs. internal systems and resources: Do you have existing systems/resources that you can

leverage for the assessment system? If so, you may be able to save the costs and retain control of the online delivery system.
  - Feasibility of using a general "best practices" vended solution to meet your specific needs: This is often feasible and can save much time and expense vs. a custom solution.
  - Your organization's willingness to rely upon a vendor to outsource HR business processes: Establishing a service-level agreement with your vendor can help to assure quality and reliability for services that your organization can count on.
- *How will the assessments be combined and used for decision-making?* Specify goals for your assessment system (e.g., candidate flow, ROI, demographic diversity) and develop criteria for scoring the assessments that are consistent with these goals.
- *How will the online assessments be deployed?* Work with IT specialists to ensure that delivery systems are available, configured properly, and well supported. Establish processes for ongoing support and maintenance, providing technical support, and fielding questions regarding test use.
- *What facilities and resources are available to deliver the assessment program?* Determine where candidates will take the tests, and who will schedule candidates and supervise testing sessions.
- *How will assessment information be maintained and integrated with other systems?* Consider how the talent acquisition program may be integrated with applicant tracking, learning management, and performance management systems.
- *What validation strategy will be used to defend the program and ensure that it is effective?* Consider the type of assessment, availability of resources (internal and external), and the time needed to conduct a validation study.
- *What are the legal risks for the assessment program and how will you prepare for them?* Consider fair employment laws, the demographic composition of your labor market, the types of assessment tools you plan to use, and the likelihood that differences in selection rates will be observed among demographic groups.
- *How will the effectiveness of the assessment program be evaluated?* Establish criteria and processes that will be used to gauge the success of your program.

Chapter 7

Tracking Tools for Staffing Managers and Recruiters

Online recruiting and staffing systems create an abundance of information about job seekers and the processes in which they participate as they explore job opportunities. Open positions are posted, job seeker information is collected, and tools for gathering evaluative information on candidates are deployed. All of these data must be maintained for presentation at the right time for recruiters, interviewers, hiring managers, and staffing specialists to draw upon to properly and efficiently execute their role in the hiring process. Most commonly, the information generated during these steps is held in one of three types of systems: the Human Resources Information System (HRIS), the applicant tracking system (ATS), or within the system that deploys screening questions, tests, and other forms of assessment. Figure 7.1 shows how these systems are frequently deployed together.

As shown in the figure, the first record of a job seeker's interest in a position will typically be tracked by the ATS. Next, job seekers may be transferred to a second system that deploys assessments such as an online testing system. Note that some organizations may have several systems integrated within their staffing process, each integrated with the ATS. During this phase, information should be maintained that tracks the users' participation in each assessment, as well as technical information about the assessment itself. Finally, once hired, the new employee information should be transferred into the company's HRIS to initiate a permanent employee record. For the purpose of

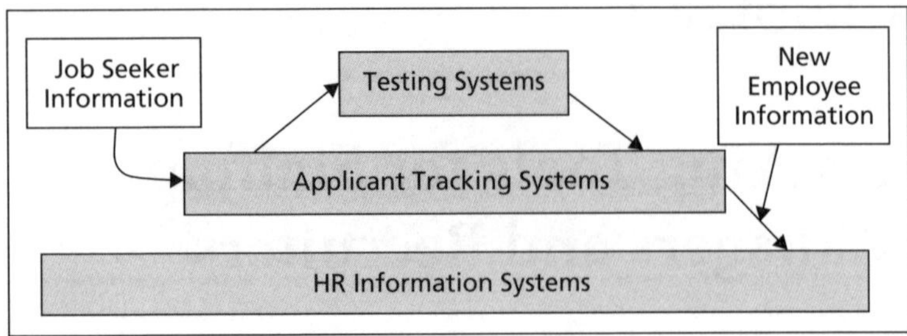

Figure 7.1 Common data tracking systems for online staffing processes

this chapter, most of the information of interest in the staffing process is held within the ATS.

A well-designed applicant tracking system (ATS) will collect and maintain information on candidates, positions, and selection processes to enable the efficient management of the recruiting and staffing functions. The ATS may also integrate job posting and background check services to further extend the value they provide to the hiring process through automation.

Aside from data tracking and management, an ATS will enable storage and reporting of candidate quality and flow information at each phase of the process. This allows for computation of metrics of system effectiveness such as the success rates of recruiters and recruiting channels, time-to-hire, and the criterion-related validity of candidate information. Data storage and reporting is also critical for understanding how the system as a whole is operating with respect to critical outcomes such as the diversity mix of the candidate pool at each stage of selection. Reports from these data also are required to support government record-keeping requirements and to respond to audit and challenge requests.

On its own, an ATS typically provides very little sophistication to support the measurement of people. The primary value of an ATS is data collection, tracking, and reporting; however, because of the centrality of the ATS to the hiring process, it serves as a backbone for a variety of other tools that may be resident within the ATS or integrated through a third-party provider. Additionally, in larger organizations the investment required to license, configure, and install an

ATS is substantial, so the other processes that are built to support selection are usually required to integrate with the ATS.

In this chapter we review the information needs of the typical roles within the staffing process, focusing primarily on the needs of recruiters, hiring managers, and staffing specialists. Although these roles are common, it is important to keep in mind that most systems allow you to configure roles within the system so that applicant information is restricted to only those users who have a business need for the data. As you configure the data tracking processes in your organization, consider which roles have a critical need for access to information, thereby reducing the risk of sensitive personal data becoming released to unauthorized users.

Information for Recruiters

Recruiters need to manage information about the recruiting process regarding both jobs and candidates. Frequently information about jobs is conveyed by a job requisition, and information about job seekers is held within a record for each candidate. Next, we examine each of these common features and configurable elements within the ATS that are designed to support recruiters.

Managing Job Requisitions

When a staffing need is created, either by adding a new position to the organization or through incumbent turnover, transfer, or promotion, the opening must be identified for the recruiters who then initiate the search for a new hire for the role. These job openings take the form of a job requisition. Requisitions are frequently used as a fundamental part of the database structure for the ATS, because they provide a method of relating job seekers to specific openings for which they will be considered. Job requisitions can be created in several ways: managers can submit a request into the ATS and create them directly, they can be submitted on paper and then manually entered by an administrator, or recruiters can create them after being informed of the opening. Once created, the requisition allows recruiters to source candidates and assign them to the requisition so that a candidate pool for the role is created.

Most of the discussion in this book has focused on the treatment of job seekers within a job requisition; however, there are some tasks that recruiters must perform that operate across requisitions. As you investigate options for configuring an ATS in your organization, consider the typical processes your recruiters perform to ensure the system can be designed to match. Common features include:

- Creation of the requisition. Ideally, new requisitions are based on models or templates that have been constructed to support the organization's job hierarchy. That is, if the new role is for an administrative assistant, a model requisition is available that shows the recommended competencies and selection steps that should be included for an administrative role in the organization. These models should be based on job analyses conducted for each job that is included in the system.
- Requisition approval. The ATS should also have tools for managing the workflow involved with getting a new requisition approved. Most organizations do not allow hiring managers and recruiters alone to create new openings and fill them. These actions should be approved by executives that own the budgets for headcount replacements and additions. The ATS should include features that trigger these approvals and track their completion.
- Candidate sourcing support. A large portion of the recruiter's job is to design and implement a sourcing strategy for each new role that will quickly fill the requisition with qualified applicants. Many ATSs include tools for automatically posting new positions with selected online job boards, such as Monster.com and CareerBuilder.com, as well as the numerous occupation-specific job sites that now exist. Much has been written about the techniques recruiters can use to find candidates via the Internet, and interested readers should consult these sources for up-to-date information about available sourcing techniques and tools.[1]
- Assignment to a job requisition. Once candidates apply, they may be placed into a specific requisition in several ways. This may happen automatically if the candidate enters the process via the organization's career page and they apply for a specific opening. The recruiter may also manually assign a candidate to a requisition. This could occur, for example, when a recruiter meets a job seeker at a college career fair. In this situation, the recruiter finds candi-

dates of interest, and assigns each of them to an appropriate requisition. The system then generates an e-mail to the candidate that includes a link into the remainder of the online staffing process. These features should also allow recruiters to move candidates across requisitions, so that even after one position is filled, viable candidates can be transferred to other requisitions for which they are qualified.

Managing Candidates

Of course, recruiters must also manage a multitude of interactions with job seekers as they enter and move through the selection process. Recruiters should be able to get quick access to available candidates and engage these candidates in the process so that the required steps can be completed at the right time. Two additional tools can help recruiters with these tasks.

- Candidate database search. Tracking systems commonly include a database for candidate information, usually populated with records of all job seekers who have indicated their interest in the company by completing an online profile or submitting a resume. If it is kept current, the candidate database has tremendous value to the organization as a source for future job candidates. Recruiters should be able to search this database using criteria that correspond to the jobs requirements. Because these searches constitute a form of selection, it is important that the system maintain a record of the search criteria that are used. For example, if the recruiter is seeking to fill an accounting role, and the role requires a degree in accounting or finance, the recruiter should be able search the education field in the database for candidates that meet this specification. The recruiter must then record the fact that these search terms were used so that the results can be re-created if necessary. Storage of search terms is now a federal reporting requirement in the United States.
- Candidate communication tools. Regular communication with job seekers is also a day-to-day activity for recruiters. The ATS should include features for automatically generating e-mail messages to candidates at various points in the recruiting process. For example, when job seekers first submit a profile on the career site, they should

receive an e-mail acknowledging their submission, ideally including a link back to their profile where they are allowed to update information or check on their progress through the selection process. Candidate communication tools that are embedded directly into the online screening site have advantages for candidate privacy and for maintaining a history of communications that can be available to recruiters each time they examine the candidate's profile. By regularly communicating with candidates about the process, the recruiter is able to keep them engaged and aware of the next steps they should complete to keep the process moving forward.

Information for Hiring Managers

The hiring manager is typically the person to whom the new hire will report. Usually he or she also makes the final hiring decision. Unlike the role of the recruiter, hiring managers typically need a streamlined and concise view of the system, so it is important that the roles within the system can be configured to prevent hiring managers from having the same level of access to information as recruiters and HR specialists. Some information, such as detailed assessment results and demographic information, should not be available to hiring managers because they are typically not trained in the proper usage of these data. Therefore tools designed for hiring managers tend to focus only on the information necessary to support their role in the process. These needs may vary in your organization depending on the extent to which managers are given broad or narrow responsibility in the hiring process.

A common hiring manager feature is a summary screen that shows the status of the candidates in the hiring process for the manager's open positions. Summary information will often include the number of applicants in the process, the number who have passed each phase, and the number who are in the queue for a final interview. Because the hiring manager conducts the final interview in most organizations, access to additional candidate information, such as the resume, online profile, results from assessments, and an interview protocol, may often be included in the hiring manager's interface. More extensive online tools are also available for structuring and facilitating the interview in accordance with the processes used throughout the organization. These tools may also be integrated within the ATS to further guide hiring managers through the process.

Information for HR Specialists

The applicant tracking system should have a variety of functions and flexibilities to accommodate a range of HR users. Typical needs for HR include administrative features, quality assurance and compliance monitoring, and strategic analytics. These features may be allocated across a variety of configured roles, or grouped together under an HR staffing specialist role. Roles are created within the system by assigning the rights to either view or write information held within different components of the ATS.

System administration roles have the broadest access to system features and data. This role should have access to an area of the system that allows a few designated users to assign user rights to other roles. It is from this role that the system security is most readily controlled. As you configure an ATS for your organization, consider who has this level of access to other related systems (e.g., performance management, benefits administration); often these roles are controlled by the HR Information Technology function. Be cautious of systems that do not allow users to manage user rights at some level. If all requests for access to available information must be handed by the people who built the ATS, it is likely the system's flexibilities will be too limited for a large organization and the cost of configuration will be higher than for systems that allow a system administrator within the client organization to set user rights.

Quality assurance and compliance monitoring is usually performed by staffing specialists within the HR function. To accommodate the needs of these users, the ATS should have standard reporting features that allow users with these rights to view applicant flow statistics (i.e., how many candidates are entering and exiting each phase of a hiring process), diversity reports (i.e., how many candidates fall into protected groups associated with race, gender, and age), and may include summary data from candidate reaction questions. (Reaction questions allow system designers to collect the opinions of job seekers about issues such as the perceived fairness of the process, the ease of use of the website, and their opinions about the specific assessments that were included.) Together these reports allow expert users of the system to evaluate and adjust selection processes to improve their efficiency, diversity, and appeal.

Strategic analytics should also be constructed as the system is initially configured. Unfortunately, the attention in the design process is mostly devoted to tactical issues related to process efficiency, but with a little more effort and foresight, the system can also be constructed to report on issues that can help your organization operate more strategically when managing talent flow. For example, information about candidate diversity and performance in the selection process can be used to determine which sources of candidates are the most productive. This can save thousands of dollars in job posting costs if it helps to steer recruiters toward the sources that are the most effective and ignoring others. Information related to the effectiveness of new hires can also be linked back to their assessments to validate their relationship to on-the-job outcomes. On a larger scale, reports that show the vacancy rates, time-to-fill, and average tenure for critical jobs in the organization can help workforce planners to project future needs in light of the business direction. It is critical that you plan for these strategic outputs from the system as it is initially configured or the necessary data may not be available once the system has been placed into operation.

Critical Issues to Resolve

As you work to select, configure, and implement an ATS to support your staffing processes, several issues must be resolved along the way. The most critical issues are related to data security and privacy and these are covered in detail in Chapter 11. Other issues can be more subtle, but if they are not addressed early in the system configuration process, they can create bigger problems as the system operates over time. A few of the issues with the biggest potential impact are reviewed here.

Integration with the ATS

As we have noted in Chapter 2, and will expand in Chapter 8, the ease with which disparate systems can be integrated into a seamless process is a concern of growing importance. Integration is a common requirement because it reduces redundancy and complexity by allowing system users to work with just one primary system and database. Integrated systems also reduce the chance that duplicate and inconsistent data exist in the HR process. And, as we will see in the next chapter, integrated HR systems can provide insights regarding the talent processes in organizations that may otherwise be obscured because the necessary data to reveal patterns, trends, and relationships are held in disparate systems.

Because the ATS plays a central role in the management of the hiring process, integration with this system is a critical factor for the overall success of your online staffing process. Figure 7.1 shows the most common integration points. For processes that include in-depth assessments, each of these assessments should be able to be efficiently integrated with the ATS, and the ATS should be designed in a manner that supports these integrations. Similar needs are present for other partners in the hiring process. Large-scale hiring systems may include separate vendors for interview support tools, in-depth assessment, background checking, and medical evaluation. Each of these processes typically requires a two-part integration: first to transfer the candidate identifier to the external vendor to trigger the vendor's process, and second to transfer the results back to the ATS so that all of the relevant data are held in a central location. Finally, the candidate record will eventually be transferred into the HRIS once the candidate has been hired.

Because of the pressure on the ATS to integrate related functions, many ATS providers, as well as HRIS providers, have started to incorporate ancillary processes into their systems. Unless your needs for these functions are very basic, you should be cautious about using the ATS or HRIS as a "one-stop shop" for such services. As the HR technology industry consolidates, larger providers are adding features and functions that mimic the basic functionality offered by specialists. However, it is technically challenging to construct a best-in-class service that can be offered for every element across a range of hiring processes. Typically only rudimentary functionality is provided within the larger systems, and organizations that wish to extend these components must eventually integrate with third-party systems anyhow. During the design phase of an ATS implementation, you will need to plan for each integration point within the staffing process. You should also investigate the ATS vendor's methods for handling future integrations. Some suggestions for the technologies to look for when considering integrations are provided in the next chapter.

Data Storage, Reporting, and Archiving

Although ATSs can track a wide range of information about job seekers and applicants, it is essential that you plan for which data elements need to be readily available to day-to-day users and which may be less easily available. We offer four guiding considerations when planning your approach to data reporting and storage.

1. *Consider if there are some data elements that you do not want to keep.* For example, some job search tools allow job seekers to examine jobs that fit their preferences, such as location, salary level, or functional area. These searches are usually conducted with an assumption of anonymity on the part of the job seeker, and the data are best left unsaved to prevent a violation of this assumption. Later, when the job seeker completes their personal profile for a specific role, questions about preferences may then be asked that can be used for assessment purposes.
2. *Consider whether some data can be packaged as exports to other systems for later processing instead of as a standard report from the system.* For example, applicants' responses to specific assessment questions may be of little relevance for immediate decision-making, so these responses may be stored and accessed quarterly for a quality check on the assessment. In this case, the response data can be made available in a downloadable database file, only to be accessed and used by an assessment expert. This reduces the cost associated with the creation of a customized report, and maintains the security of sensitive information.
3. *Determine whether the ATS reporting function can provide your users with the flexibility to handle infrequent data queries.* For example, a recruiting team that handles a huge seasonal influx of candidates for a specific role may want to examine their candidate lists only by the date of their application. Other recruiting teams may prefer a standard report that shows all candidates that have applied to a particular requisition; for them, partitioning by date would only obscure the bigger picture. In this case, the recruiters with the higher volume may be handled through the use of a search tool that allows them to pick from a variety of search criteria to generate more restricted views of their candidate pool.

4. *Consider how long the data should remain active within the system.* For most recruiting purposes, the data generated during the application process declines in value over time. Candidates move, their education level and experience changes and their assessment scores become less relevant. Jobs also change over time. For these reasons, the candidates that entered your organization's database several years ago will only distract your users from the candidates that are actively interested in new jobs right now. Because online recruiting processes can quickly generate tens of thousands of applicants, the ability to archive candidate records when they reach a predefined "expiration" date is important for maintaining the vitality of the system. Many systems will allow for old records to be moved to a portion of the database that is not available to regular users. It is also important that these records can still be accessed by administrators in case they are needed for legal, audit, or other recordkeeping purposes.

ATS Customization vs. Configuration

The recruiting and hiring process in large organizations can be complex. Many individual users, each playing an important role in the process, need current information to perform their part. The automated systems that support these roles are also complex. Another inevitable issue occurs when people systems and technology systems do not align.

If you find that not all of your organization's recruiting processes are modeled in the software you are implementing, you must consider whether to change current processes to fit what is possible within the software or to request a change to the software so it will better map into your current business processes. As you deliberate this balance, recognize that software changes can be expensive, and you can run the risk of forcing your software provider to create a custom version of their tool for your company. Customization is usually an undesirable outcome because maintenance and upgrade costs are substantial for custom software. Therefore only those recruiting processes that are fundamental to your business operations should be forced into the software. Fortunately, many tracking systems include a range of configurable features that allow the standard software platform to conform to a range of business processes. On the other hand, if your recruiting practices are unique and essential to your business operations, you may also consider having a custom system built specifically for your organization. For most organizations the cost of this approach will outweigh the benefits. We will return to this option in the next chapter.

A summary of the best practices reviewed in this chapter, as well as the realities often faced during the implementation of tracking systems, is provided in the box below.

Best Practices and Realities:

Configuration and Implementation of Applicant Tracking Systems

Best Practices

- The roles within the ATS are carefully planned so that each participant in the hiring process has ready access to the information they need to fulfill their role in the process.
- Candidate information can be readily updated when appropriate.
- Recruiter information is assembled in a manner that reflects their work processes; the workflow is efficient.
- Manager access is limited to the information they need to understand the progress of candidates through the system and to conduct informed interviews.
- The ATS allows for a wide range of options for configuring additional HR roles. Pre-designed reports provide easy access to information that is critical for monitoring the selection process.
- The ATS is fully integrated with the HRIS and various assessment providers' systems.
- Strategic reports (e.g., predicted vacancy rates) are planned in advance.

Realities

- ATS systems frequently cannot be configured to existing business processes. Participants in the process are forced to accommodate some aspects of the system that were envisioned only by its designers.
- Some users will only partially complete information within the ATS. This limits the effectiveness of the overall system; for example, some system reports won't make sense owing to missing information.
- Integration across systems can become complex and expensive because various vendors have used different approaches to their system interfaces. Some processes are then used in a disconnected and inefficient manner.
- The ATS is initially configured to optimize efficiency, and critical information that may be relevant for longer-term talent strategy is overlooked.

Chapter 8

Systems Design and Integration

Since we last checked in with Sandra, she has made substantial progress on the plans for her new online staffing system. So far, the process for identifying the right tools to include in the new process has been guided by Sandra's high-level vision and guidance for what the system should do. In short, Sandra wanted the following elements:

- A Careers page that is connected to the XYZ corporate website. The page must describe the company and job opportunities in an accurate but highly engaging manner.
- An automated application and screening process that can be configured to fit any job in the company.
- A few assessments that have been validated for selecting candidates in several job families.
- An integrated background checking service, so that applicants who pass all parts of the selection process can be immediately forwarded for a background check.
- A new applicant tracking system (ATS) that will capture all of the information from this process and transfer the results to XYZ's existing HR information system.

Working with a small team of internal experts and a consultant she designed a storyboard layout for the new process. At first this started as a series of flipcharts that Sandra and her team prepared in a design meeting; then the process was rendered by a graphics specialist to look like a series of web pages. This prototype effectively solidified the views of the team toward a common vision.

Now the team is taking the next steps toward implementation. Partners have been selected for the ATS and for the different assessments that were envisioned. Validation studies for the assessments are getting under way. The current challenge for the team is to plan the detailed system design and the integration points between the various elements that make up the new online staffing process for XYZ. The technical specialists on her team begin their work at this point in the project. Sandra assumes that her high-level vision for the system would continue to guide the implementation; however, she finds that the team still needs her involvement in several decisions as the technical details are worked out. Sandra feels out of her element as the technical discussions ensue, but as the conversations progress she begins to see the logic of how the pieces of her system will come together. She realizes some implications of the system that she had not considered deeply yet: new computer hardware requirements, changes to the company firewall, and user support services all had to be planned. Also, the methods by which her new partners (an assessment company, a background check service, and an ATS provider) were going to integrate their systems had to be worked out.

Effective integration between the various components of the process is important for Sandra. If the assessment tools, the ATS, and HRIS are not all connected in a way that makes the process efficient and seamless, she worries that the new process won't be seen as any different than the disconnected tools that XYZ currently uses. She knows that if the parts of her model are not automated and connected, hiring managers in the company won't use them consistently – too much effort and responsibility to follow a process always seems to lead to inconsistency and chaos at XYZ. Sandra also has a longer-term goal for the system: if the parts are properly integrated, she can use information across the components to monitor and report on their whole staffing process. This will allow her to report back to XYZ's executive team in ways that draw them into discussions about staffing and talent management on a whole new level.

At this point in the implementation process, Sandra is most concerned with how the technical design and integration will be done.

If this portion is successful, she feels that she can then rally the organization, and her executive team, behind the whole project. Her team follows the steps described in this chapter to plan the design and integration of the system.

* * *

Key Elements for System Design

Assembling an integrated online staffing system requires careful planning. Asking the right questions in advance will pay dividends by ensuring that the system is built to align with your business needs and that it operates smoothly, efficiently, and securely. A useful approach to system design is outlined in Figure 8.1. Begin by identifying the vision and goals for the system, and the business requirements and functions to be addressed. From there, you can start by working with technology experts to translate business goals and requirements into technical specifications for core elements of the system, including the architectural structure and the envisioned "nuts and bolts" (actually boxes and wires) infrastructure of the system.

Figure 8.1 System planning and design process

Design Elements

Following is an outline of key system design elements and a brief discussion of each one to provide you with an idea of what to expect in the planning process and what questions to ask providers of these system components.

- *Vision and goals:* Start by establishing the reasons for building the system and examining the costs and benefits of undertaking such a project. Then identify the critical goals that the system should be designed to accomplish (e.g., reducing candidate cycle time, reducing cost per hire, providing real-time information to enable management of the talent pipeline and key metrics for performance).

- *Functional business requirements:* Identify and document the various ways that the system will be used to accomplish organizational goals (e.g., posting jobs to job boards, collecting applications, conducting screening and testing). Document the sequence of steps that users will follow in accessing and navigating the system and its various functions. Specify all of the inputs, processes, and outputs within and between systems. The end result will be a series of flow charts and descriptions of what the system should do and how it should work; often the requirements will be drawn as a storyboard view of how the system should flow. This document will serve as a touchstone throughout the project to ensure that the requirements are fulfilled.
- *Architecture requirements:* Your technical experts will be the leaders of this component, which will entail translating business requirements into the architectural design and technical requirements for the system. Specifications for hardware, software, connectivity and networking, and database management will also be defined at this stage. A simplified system architecture is shown in Figure 8.2, which graphically depicts major components and how they are related. In this example, remote users at individual computer stations access the system over the Internet and must have credentials to pass through a system firewall. A load balancer detects system activity relative to capacity and diverts traffic between two completely redundant systems, which are operated by a third-party vendor as

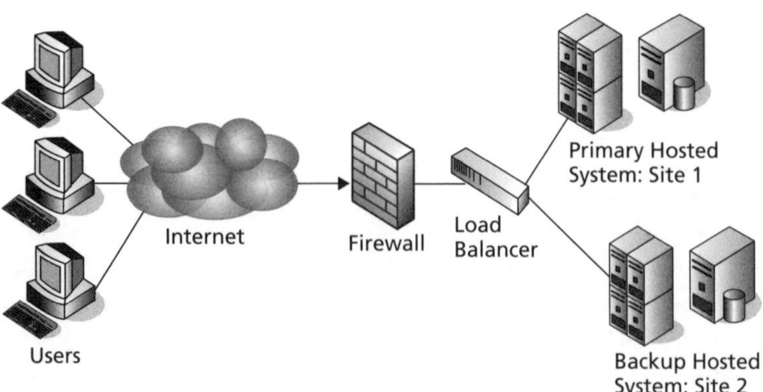

Figure 8.2 Example system architecture diagram

a hosted system. The redundant systems also serve as a backup to preserve business continuity in the event that one system fails.

- *Software requirements:* Among the technical requirements, your experts must determine the software required to access and operate the online staffing system. Many systems operate under an Application Service Provider (ASP) model over the Internet, which requires only a web browser (e.g., Microsoft Internet Explorer) for users to receive on-demand services. Some systems may require users to download "plug-in" software modules in order to work (e.g., Java or ActiveX). It will also be important to determine the capability the system will have to integrate with other systems. Is the system compliant with XML and other tools that facilitate integration?
- *Infrastructure:* The system infrastructure draws from the architecture, technical requirements, and specifications. Your IT experts will identify specific types of hardware, software, and networks that will be used, as well as data locations, firewalls, security provisions, and other details needed to deploy the system. During this phase of planning, you should ask for alternative infrastructure plans that will enable you to evaluate costs for acquisition, installation, maintenance, and support, as well as system capacity, scalability (expansion capability), compatibility with other systems, and vendor quality and support.

Finally, it is important to plan for the operational support that will be required to keep the system running smoothly once it is fully implemented. Several areas of support should be planned:

- *Host system requirements:* It is common for HR systems to be hosted by third-party vendors that specialize in providing the required hardware and technical support to operate large web-based systems. Identify any capacity limitations of the hosting system, such as number of concurrent users, database storage, and numbers and types of assessments that can be delivered. Also, determine how reliable the system is – what is the average "uptime" (percentage of time available in a twenty-four-hour period)? When is the regular maintenance scheduled and how will users be notified of system unavailability?
- *User system requirements:* Determine the computer system requirements (hardware, software, connectivity) for all types of users

(e.g., recruiters, candidates, administrators, hiring managers) to access the online staffing system.

- *Technical support:* Determine the technical support needed for administrative users and technology staff to configure and maintain user systems. Who will provide support, by what means will it be provided, and during what hours will it be available?
- *Disaster recovery:* Identify backup systems and processes that will "kick-in" if the primary online service is disrupted. Confirm processes for data preservation, protection and recovery in the event of a catastrophic event. A plan should be documented specifying how the continuity of business operations will be maintained.
- *Security:* Specifications for system security should be established and documented, including physical hardware protection, software access, database integrity, and screening of personnel who have access to the system. (See Chapter 11 for a more detailed discussion of data security issues.)

Integration Concepts and Approaches

One of the most powerful advantages of online staffing systems is the capability to integrate processes and information. By linking automated processes such as recruitment, applicant tracking, and assessment, you can significantly improve the efficiency of HR operations in your organization, while consolidating HR information to provide a dashboard view of your staffing program. An integrated HR Information System enables you to monitor and continuously improve operational effectiveness, while managing the talent pipeline in your organization.

Earlier in Chapter 2 we reviewed key drivers and business trends that fueled the push to integrate HR component systems, along with software tools, processes, and models that are available to facilitate integration. In the remainder of this chapter we review the essential concepts and considerations for designing and implementing integrated HR systems, including:

- basic concepts and approaches to integrating online HR systems;
- critical issues that you are likely to face in system design and integration.

Two primary reasons for integrating component systems are to enable automated transition between different processes, and to link information that is generated in different systems. While there are a variety of approaches to accomplishing these goals, a simplified framework for thinking about integration methods is to view them in two broad classes. One class of methods focuses on exchanging *instructions* between systems. These methods enable one system to invoke functions in another system in a manner that creates the impression to users that they are operating within a single system (i.e., transitions between different systems appear seamless). The other class of integration methods enables the exchange of *information* between systems to support both operational and strategic processes. The most sophisticated systems incorporate both approaches.

Linking Processes – Exchanging Instructions between Systems

Approaches to integrating functionality between systems vary in scope and complexity for addressing functions such as execution of business rules, data management, security, and system recovery capabilities. Two approaches that illustrate the range of alternatives are: (1) system-to-system messaging and (2) web services.

System-to-system messaging. Under this simple approach, one system sends a request message to another system. The message could be to start a remote software application, get data, or some other request. Simple Object Access Protocol (SOAP) is a widely used convention for system-to-system messaging to enable operations between systems (interoperability). An international consortium of organizations and working groups, the World Wide Web Consortium (W3C), maintains the SOAP specification. The W3C website is an excellent source for background information on system interoperability specifications.[1]

An example of HR system integration via system-to-system messaging is described in the box overleaf. In this example, a hidden URL ("hyperlink") is embedded in the software application, which directs the candidate's computer to another system and launches another

Good to Know:

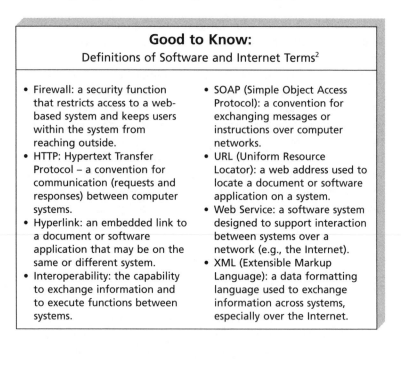

Definitions of Software and Internet Terms[2]

- Firewall: a security function that restricts access to a web-based system and keeps users within the system from reaching outside.
- HTTP: Hypertext Transfer Protocol – a convention for communication (requests and responses) between computer systems.
- Hyperlink: an embedded link to a document or software application that may be on the same or different system.
- Interoperability: the capability to exchange information and to execute functions between systems.
- SOAP (Simple Object Access Protocol): a convention for exchanging messages or instructions over computer networks.
- URL (Uniform Resource Locator): a web address used to locate a document or software application on a system.
- Web Service: a software system designed to support interaction between systems over a network (e.g., the Internet).
- XML (Extensible Markup Language): a data formatting language used to exchange information across systems, especially over the Internet.

Example Integration between HR Systems:

System-to-System Messaging and Information Exchange

A prospective job candidate visits an employer's recruitment website and reviews various job opportunities. The prospect indicates an interest in applying for a position by clicking "Apply Now" and a hidden hyperlink (https://jobapplication.com) transparently redirects the candidate's computer to an online job application on a system hosted by Vendor A. When the application is completed, the qualified candidate is given the option to complete an online assessment of work attitudes. If the candidate clicks "Yes" a hidden hyperlink (https://sampletest.com/companyID.password) seamlessly redirects the candidate's computer to an assessment system hosted by Vendor B. At the conclusion of the assessment the candidate's computer is redirected to the employer's website and the candidate's assessment results are automatically transmitted in encrypted XML format to a central database hosted by the applicant tracking system. Administrative users of the ATS are able to view candidate information and assessment results on demand.

application, forming a chain of software applications that create the impression of a single system. At the conclusion of each application, additional requests and responses may be transmitted between systems. In the example from XYZ Corp. presented at the start of this chapter, the integration between the automated application process and the assessment system could be developed just as the example in the box below describes.

There are several advantages of the system-to-system messaging method of integration: it is relatively quick and easy to develop and implement, it can be used in a variety of applications, and it requires little investment in resources for software development and implementation. Disadvantages include limited functional capabilities, limitations on the amount of data that can be sent, and slower processing when large messages are transmitted. An example of these limitations occurs when errors are encountered. In the event of system failure (e.g., due to hardware, software, or connectivity problems) when a candidate is using the second system in a chain, how will the first system detect, respond and recover from the problem? Will it recognize that the user had a problem and place them back to where they left off? Or, will the system start over at the beginning (often to the frustration and confusion of the user)? Integration processes that have less functional capability tend to require more technical support for users which is another potential disadvantage.

Web services. A powerful method for integrating web-based staffing systems is the use of web services. As we discussed in Chapter 2, web services are essentially independent software modules that can be seamlessly integrated with other systems so that they operate together as a single system. Web services can act as a sort of mediator to enable different systems, based on different programming languages, to easily share a component of software functionality. Once a web service is developed, it is reusable and can be configured with minimal effort, with the aim of avoiding the cost and time associated with software customization.

In the XYZ system example, the company that conducts background checks would benefit from a web services approach. By creating a reusable access point to their system, the background check company could easily integrate with multiple companies' staffing systems using the same web service. Other examples of web services that support integration include: protocols for enhanced security, reliable messaging between systems, error handling, and restarting interrupted sessions.

Web services offer several advantages, including enhanced system interoperability (e.g., for error handling, backup, and recovery capabilities), more reliable operation, and thus, potentially fewer user support calls. Also, because they are consistent with the emerging best practice of service-oriented architecture (SOA), web services provide a means for staffing components to be integrated into HRISs and other systems that support talent management processes. This capability is an enormous advantage because it provides the opportunity to link critical functions such as recruitment, selection, training, and performance management, thereby enabling new operational efficiencies and revealing information that can help facilitate strategic planning in areas such as workforce gaps, training needs, and succession planning.

Perhaps the biggest potential disadvantage to web service-based integration is that it can be more time- and resource-intensive to develop the initial web service program; however, once developed, the component can be reused in other applications that need the service.

Linking Data – Exchanging Information between Systems

In the example of the system that Sandra is implementing at XYZ there are some integration points where one system merely provides information to another, such as when a successful applicant's information is transferred into XYZ's HRIS to create an employee record. In this case, only the name, identification number, and selected assessment results might need to be transferred to the HRIS; all additional data can be stored in the ATS if it is needed in the future.

As in any form of communication, success in integrating data between different systems is made possible by adopting a common language. Extensible Markup Language (XML) is a widely recognized standard for information exchange, enabling software providers to use a common language to transfer data between systems.[3] XML uses indicators (called "tags") to define each data element and these are embedded in the file itself, so there is no need to transmit separate instructions for processing the information (as long as each software provider agrees to use the common language).

For example, the computer language can be as simple as the following:

<TestScore> 92 </TestScore>

This line of code states that a piece of information is being transferred and it is a test score (<TestScore>). The score itself (92) is then provided, and the final portion of the XML tag (</TestScore>) tells the receiving system that the score information has been completed.

Need for standards. Adopting a common language has the potential to dramatically streamline the integration process between disparate systems. However, there is a major vulnerability in the process that can still create barriers to integration: XML and similar tools are highly flexible, and different terms and phrases can be used to mean the same thing. For example, if different software developers use different terms to describe common data elements and processes, the integration between systems still must be negotiated at a highly detailed level. If one system uses "<TestScore>" and another system uses "<T_Score>" to represent the same information, the system language must still be reconciled before integration of the systems can occur.

To reduce the risks that this flexibility can bring, a number of industry consortium groups have been established to define standard terms that should be used to convey common information and processes within a market. These consortium groups meet to decide on what data elements should be described in common terms and what those terms should be. As long as the system designers all adhere to the standards set by the consortium, then integration between systems is dramatically simplified owing to the benefits of a common language that governs information transfer.

The specific application of XML in HR and assessment systems has been addressed by two organizations. The HR-XML consortium was organized by major HR software companies to address the need for standards in system interoperability for a range of HR functions, such as assessment, background checks, resume processing, and payroll. Core specifications for transmitting these data are published by the HR-XML consortium and may be accessed at the consortium's website.[4] Another organization, the IMS Global Learning Consortium, has also published standard specifications for system interoperability, specifically with regard to test questions and test data.[5]

Tips

Integrate systems by ...	*When ...*
Exchanging instructions	It is important to create the impression that the functions in different systems are operating within a single system. For example, when it is desirable to have a single login or private labeled or branded initial access.
Exchanging information	It is important to aggregate data across systems. For example, when it is desirable to have data from multiple systems reside in one location to enable evaluation and reporting or strategic program management.

Critical Issues to Resolve

Once you have completed initial planning and specifications for your integrated staffing system and begin to contemplate implementation, there are several important issues that you will need to address. These include:

- *Buy or build?* Conduct a cost–benefit analysis to determine whether it is feasible for you to develop a proprietary system that can serve some or all of your staffing needs, or whether it makes more sense for you to use a vended solution. Some organizations have developed their own job application systems, which integrate with more sophisticated vendor systems for applicant tracking, screening, or assessment. A key consideration for your cost–benefit analysis is whether internal resources are available which may be leveraged to design, develop, implement, support, and maintain an online staffing system, including software, hardware, and assessment instruments. In addition to weighing the financial costs, it is also important to consider development cycle time and expertise requirements to undertake the development of a home-grown online staffing system.

- *How will the system impact existing business processes?* A classic issue that emerges when organizations adopt new automated staffing systems is whether changes in business processes will be required in order to fit the software. Organizations often discover that their business processes are not standard and, in the process of establishing standards, often get caught up in redesigning them. Also, software programs will usually offer a range of configurable options that encompass common business practices, but they may not cover yours, so you may be faced with a decision: customize the software or change business processes. Like many business issues, the answer typically falls in the middle and requires some of both.
- *Implementation planning.* You will need to work with a range of subject matter experts: IT specialists to design, develop, and maintain hardware systems; software developers to code and maintain staffing software programs; workplace psychologists to develop and validate assessment tools; and an operations manager to facilitate the delivery of services and technical support. Establishing a close working relationship with an IT expert and advisor is particularly important to ensure that the system is both technically sound and will meet your needs. To this end, it will be beneficial for you to become familiar with technology terminology and concepts, establish and communicate a clear vision of your objectives for the system, and to be an active partner in the system design.
- *Planning for growth and change.* Like the organizations they serve, staffing systems are dynamic and must be designed to accommodate changing needs and requirements. In addition, hardware and software technology is continuously evolving and upgrades will be periodically required, as changes in operating systems and hosting environments are updated. The system should be designed to be scalable to accommodate growth in capacity and functionality. Avoiding extensive customization of the system and instead relying upon configurable options that can be easily changed will foster efficient evolution of the system in the long run.

* * *

Let's look in on Sandra one last time. Her team has now completed the development of the XYZ system and the hard work for Sandra really begins. Her task now is to socialize the use of the system into the organization to ensure that it is rolled out and used appropriately. Like any organizational change, the effective implementation of XYZ's staffing system will depend not only on a well-designed technical system, but also on Sandra's executive capabilities. She sets out to clearly communicate the expectations for the users, to align resources, define accountabilities, and build the skills of those who will use the system on a regular basis. Sandra also defines several measures of success for the system, such as an improved average time-to-hire and higher-quality hires, as measured by a new-hire survey that she plans to implement.

As the system rolls through its first few months of operation, several new issues emerge that Sandra and her team must address. These issues include whether the assessments can be given to professional candidates who might take them from home, whether the process can be used at the XYZ plants that are located outside of the United States, and how the security of the system should be maintained. We examine these issues in greater detail in the next section of the book.

Part III

Consequences and Issues Associated with Online Deployment

Chapter 9

Managing the Environment

Armed with the right assessment tools and a well-designed online delivery system, you are ready to implement your talent assessment program. What can go wrong? As it turns out, plenty. Even the most well-designed assessment tools and delivery systems can be marred by extraneous factors that emerge during implementation. As we saw in Chapter 3, administration conditions can affect the quality of measurement and, if unchecked, result in less reliable and valid information upon which to base your talent decisions. Successful deployment of talent assessment programs requires careful attention to the conditions under which the system will operate.

Good operating conditions are especially important when the stakes are high. This principle is well known in professional sports, for example, where much is at risk for the owners and players – money, careers, publicity, and historical records. When a high-stakes game is affected by a rule violation or unfair condition (bad call, broken time clock, cheating), it can become a source of controversy, sometimes reaching national attention and even congressional investigations (as was the case with the use of performance-enhancing drugs in baseball). Accordingly, extreme care is devoted to standardizing, preparing, and managing the game conditions to ensure that the players are able to perform at their best under standard conditions, and that the outcome of the contest is fair.

In the same manner, it is important to ensure that online assessment programs are implemented under appropriate conditions so that measures of job candidate capabilities and qualities are accurate and fair, especially if the information is used to support high-stakes employment decisions. To this end, we have the same concerns about standards, preparation, and management of the administration of online assessments. In this chapter, we review a variety of issues and challenges that emerge when deploying online assessment systems.

> **Example:**
> Managing Environmental Conditions
>
> Professional sports
>
> - *Standards:* Rules of the game are well defined, including the field dimensions, equipment, and acceptable player behavior.
> - *Preparation:* The groundskeeper ensures proper field conditions; equipment manager ensures player gear meets specifications.
> - *Management:* Referees, umpires, judges ensure that all standards are followed; industry associations and commissioner provide oversight.
>
> Online assessment systems
>
> - *Standards:* Professional standards and legal guidelines for testing and the use of selection procedures outline key concerns for implementation that may affect measurement quality and fairness.
> - *Preparation:* Program administrators, proctors, IT specialists, and others ensure appropriate test facilities and procedures, hardware, software, connectivity, etc.
> - *Management:* Proctors and program administrators ensure that standards are followed; oversight is made by regulatory agencies (legal) and senior management (return on investment).

Ensuring Quality in the Deployment of Online Staffing Systems

Professional practice standards have long called for standardized procedures for test administration in a suitable environment with efforts to preserve the integrity of the assessment system. The concern is that variations and problems with environmental and administrative conditions may create unwanted effects on candidate performance, perceptions, and participation in the assessment process. As the use of Internet-based testing has increased, there has been a growing recognition that even more careful attention should be paid to administrative and environmental conditions that have become more complex as the options for test administration have increased. The use of technology in assessment delivery raises new issues and has spurred an increased interest in alternative test delivery models (e.g., self-service, unproctored administration). Researchers and practitioners have begun to explore the issues raised by Internet-based testing; however, this work is still evolving.[1]

Issues and Challenges

The primary goal of assessment is to obtain accurate information about candidates to enable good talent decisions. There are a variety of deployment-related issues that raise potential measurement concerns that are particularly relevant to online testing. These issues are inter-dependent and one can certainly spur and intensify the others:

- proctored vs. unproctored administration;
- nonstandard testing environment;
- variations in technology;
- security problems;
- cheating;
- unqualified applicants;
- candidate differences in access to online assessment;
- candidate experience and perceptions of the assessment process.

Although this list may seem daunting, these potential issues can be avoided or mitigated with careful planning and execution. An outline of suggested strategies for addressing these issues is presented at the end of this chapter.

Good to Know:
Standards and Guidelines for Test Administration Conditions

- *Standards for Educational and Psychological Testing.* Identifies the need to address cheating, "stand-ins," equal treatment, and the testing environment (Standards 5.4, 5.6, 7.12, 8.7).
- *Principles for the Validation and Use of Employee Selection Procedures.* Identifies the need for security, standardization of testing conditions, candidate authentication, and accessibility of testing (pp. 40, 55, 56).
- *International Guidelines on Computer-Based and Internet Delivered Testing.*[2] Identifies the need to address technology, psychometric quality, levels of testing supervision, and security.
- *Guidelines for Computer-Based Testing.*[3] Identifies the need to address technology design, development, test administration, scoring, psychometric analysis, communications, and security.

Proctored vs. Unproctored Administration

One of the first planning points in test implementation is to determine where the assessments will take place and how they will be administered. Traditionally, tests have been administered at an employer's office and the sessions conducted by trained proctors who confirm the identity of the candidate, provide instructions, and monitor candidates to prevent cheating, copying, or loss of test materials. The advent of web-delivered assessments has led many businesses to question the need for onsite proctored administration and some have adopted unproctored Internet-based testing (UIT), allowing candidates to take an assessment when and wherever they choose. To some, UIT is a logical step in the direction of self-service HR and the outsourcing or elimination of traditional HR administrative functions, and is consistent with the increasing trend for remote offices and "teleworking." Other organizations that are new to assessment may simply lack the necessary infrastructure and be tempted to adopt UIT as an easy low-cost entrée into talent assessment.

There must be a catch – why aren't all employers using UIT? There is, of course, and the reasons include the issues listed in the following sections. To date there has been little research on the effects of UIT on the quality, effectiveness, and security of assessment programs, and even less professional agreement with regard to acceptable and ethical practice in this area. Proponents of UIT often cite e-commerce and high-stakes financial transactions that occur over the Internet on a daily basis as an argument for UIT. However, online fraud rates and revenue losses are not mentioned, which are estimated to cost businesses billions per year – an estimated $3.6 billion in 2007 according to the CyberSpace 9th Annual Fraud Report.[4] Distance e-learning programs were the among the first to adopt UIT and, with the longest track record of use in this relatively new practice area, are leading efforts to manage the security of remote testing programs with remote proctoring techniques and technologies (e.g., video, thumbprints and other biometrics).

When UIT is adopted, conservative practices are generally advised which appear to pose the least risk to measurement in employment settings, such as:

- low-stakes use (e.g., low or no screening hurdle; not a sole selection criterion);
- non-cognitive assessment (where cheating is presumed to pose less risk compared to cognitive ability and skill tests);
- controlled access (e.g., restricting access to known candidates).

A Range of Proctoring Scenarios[5]

- *Managed delivery:* This is the highest level of supervision and control over the test-taking environment, normally achieved by the use of dedicated testing centers where there is a high level of control over authentication, access, security, the qualification of test administration staff, and the quality and technical specifications of the test equipment.
- *Supervised delivery:* In this mode test-taker identity can be authenticated and there is a degree of direct supervision over test taking. For example, an administrator may login a candidate and confirm that the test had been properly administered and completed.
- *Controlled delivery:* No direct authentication or supervision of the assessment session is involved; the test is made available only to known test-takers. For example, test-takers may be required to obtain a logon username and password, and/or provide basic qualifying information.
- *Open access:* Not typically used for assessment, this mode allows the test to be accessed via the Internet from any location with no authentication of the test-taker and no direct supervision of the assessment session.

When planning where and how your online assessment program will be implemented, there is a range of scenarios from which to choose. The box on page 137 describes four basic levels of proctoring. Keep in mind that the higher the degree of control over testing location, access, authentication, and supervision of the testing session, the greater the integrity of the program and the information it yields, as well as the opportunity to provide a positive candidate experience.

Test Environment Issues

A concern with test environment conditions is that they may vary within and across testing locations where some examinees may not have adequate facilities. Factors such as noise, equipment, lighting, and ergonomic conditions (work space, temperature, air quality) can potentially distract candidates during the assessment and affect their performance and their perceptions of the assessment program. There has been little published research on the effects of environmental conditions (at the time of this writing), although one recent study reported that candidates' environment perceptions were associated with their assessment scores, suggesting that at best, candidates who scored well tended to view the testing environment more favorably than those who scored lower; and at worst, testing environment problems caused candidates to perform less well on assessments than candidates who reported no problems.[6] In either case, the implication is that ensuring a good environment for testing is important to the success of online assessment programs. In addition to ensuring that there are no barriers to good test performance, fostering a positive candidate experience is important to the organization's image and may make a difference in the competition for top talent.

To this end, it is good practice to routinely monitor the test environment using a variety of methods, such as giving a survey to candidates immediately following the online assessment to capture their reactions and ratings of the test conditions. This will not only provide you with program quality-control data to manage testing operations, but will also prove to be helpful in resolving complaints about the assessment delivery and claims that environment problems affected their test performance.

Technology Issues

Similar to the physical testing environment, computer systems that deliver online assessments may vary in quality and standards, potentially creating the same unwanted effects (variation in test performance that is not related to the test itself, and negative candidate perceptions of the process). When computer systems are operated and maintained by professionals under supervised conditions, technology problems can be held to a minimum. At the other end of the continuum, in UIT programs there may be literally thousands of different local systems that are operating under widely different configurations that may not be up to date, and which may not work well with your online system even if it is extremely flexible. Examples of technology delivery issues to consider include:

- *Computer hardware impacts how candidates see and respond to questions:* For example, improper display monitor settings may result in an incomplete view of the assessment; an old computer may respond very slowly; a wireless mouse or keyboard may be unreliable when answering questions.
- *Local operating software impacts how candidates access the online testing system:* For example, the web browser software may be outdated or incompatible with the online assessment system and this may cause problems with the appearance, navigation, or functioning of the test.
- *Internet connectivity impacts how candidates navigate and respond to the test:* For example, a slow or unstable Internet connection may cause problems ranging from a frustrating candidate experience owing to slow "screen paints," to loss of testing time, to disruption of the testing session and loss of candidate responses.

Given the potential for technology trouble, it is advisable to develop user system guidelines that can be distributed in advance of the assessment session to help ensure that local hardware and software are configured properly to work with your system. Depending upon the scope of your online system, your IT team will likely need to provide documentation and support to IT staff at remote locations of your organization, particularly during roll-out of the initial program. To support a UIT program, a "tech support" help desk is highly recommended to assist remote unsupported users with common system configuration issues (e.g., web browser settings; enabling "applets"; updating software versions; resuming "broken" sessions).

Security Issues

Security has long been an important concern for all modes of assessment delivery, regardless of the technology employed. With online staffing systems, security concerns are heightened because of increased capabilities to access and distribute copyrighted content and to access information about people in an automated database. Organizations run the risk that intellectual property and personal information may be lost, stolen, or inadvertently distributed. In addition to the risk of hiring unqualified people who have access to compromised test material (see *Cheating*, below), there are other potentially severe consequences of a security breach, including the costs to replace intellectual property, compromised content and results of the assessment program, and damage to the reputation and credibility of the organization. The key challenge is to deploy online staffing programs in a manner that protects information and minimizes these risks. Data security issues are explored in greater depth in Chapter 11.

Cheating

Also related to security is the specific concern that examinees may resort to a variety of unauthorized means to artificially increase their scores, and in the process, compromise the security of the assessment content. Cheating has always been a concern with high-stakes assessment programs, even before the availability of online delivery. Estimates of the base rate for cheating vary, but the consensus is that cheating on standardized tests is a pervasive problem. For example, it is estimated that well over 50% of students have cheated on exams, which does not bode well for employers who ultimately select from this future workforce.[7] Concerns with cheating are exacerbated by online testing, where additional opportunities and methods for inflating test scores may occur.

A variety of scenarios for cheating in high-stakes conditions are possible, depending upon the deployment model, and is certainly of greatest concern with UIT. Some key concerns include:

- Candidate authentication: who's taking the test? Candidates may use stand-ins to complete the test, or obtain assistance from other people during the test.
- Use of aids, such as calculators, spell-checkers, and reference books.
- Copying or taking a picture of the test may not only help a candidate improve his or her score, but could potentially expose the test content to many people.
- Practicing the test by stopping and restarting, or logging in under different names before the "real" attempt.

Despite potential cheating concerns, utility is gained in assessment by eliminating a percentage of "unqualified" candidates. Cheating-related errors in selection decisions (false positives – allowing unqualified people to pass) might be addressed in a variety of ways (retesting, verification) or presumed to be small and of no practical significance. One view is that the impact of cheating is parallel to that of faking on personality measures. That is, although it is possible to cheat (fake), in practice most people refrain from cheating (faking) and validity and decision-making are largely unaffected by cheating (faking).[8]

There is some encouraging research to suggest that the potential impact of cheating on validity and selection decisions would be small under certain conditions. For example, when a low cut score is used (e.g., screening out 16% of candidates) on a test battery with high validity, the base rate for cheating is relatively low (e.g., less than 10% of examinees cheat), and score inflation due to cheating is moderate (e.g., one standard deviation or less), it is estimated that the percentage of people passing due to cheating would be 1.4%. When the cut score is set higher (e.g., screening out 50% of candidates) under the same conditions, the percentage of people passing due to cheating is estimated to be 3.5%.[9] The CyberSpace Fraud report indicated that less than 2% of online commercial transactions were fraudulent. If this represents the "honesty rate" among online job applications, that would be good news. The problem is, we do not know the base rates for cheating on employment tests under different deployment conditions, and the effects of cheating on testing and decision-making can be very substantial when the cheat rate and score inflation are high.

Unqualified Applicants

Ease of access to online systems is a two-edged sword. On the one side, it may increase the flow of candidates through the recruitment pipeline; on the other, it may result in a larger pool of unqualified candidates who might take assessments out of curiosity or convenience more than genuine interest and suitability for the position. A concern is that casting a broader net in recruitment creates the potential for the assessment to become a problem when less well targeted candidate pools result in lower passing rates. This may increase risk for the organization if many applicants from legally protected demographic groups do not pass. Noteworthy in this regard are the legal requirements for tracking job applicants, as we discussed in Chapters 3 and 7, which specifically include online applications for purposes of monitoring the impact of selection procedures upon demographic groups. A key implication for deployment of online assessments is to ensure that candidates meet basic qualifications before allowing access to testing tools.

Access to Technology

Another potential issue associated with technology-based assessment is the difference among demographic groups in their access to computers and Internet technology – the "digital divide." As we discussed in Chapter 1, substantial differences in home access to the Internet have been found among racial/ethnic, age, and socio-economic groups, according to studies by the U.S. Department of Commerce, National Telecommunications and Information Administration[10] and the Pew Internet and American Life Project.[11] These differences are illustrated in Figure 9.1. It is encouraging that despite a lower Internet usage rate, minorities have been found to rely on the Internet for job searches at a relatively high rate, regardless of whether they have at-home access. Nevertheless, the concern with online staffing systems is that group differences in Internet usage might impact candidate

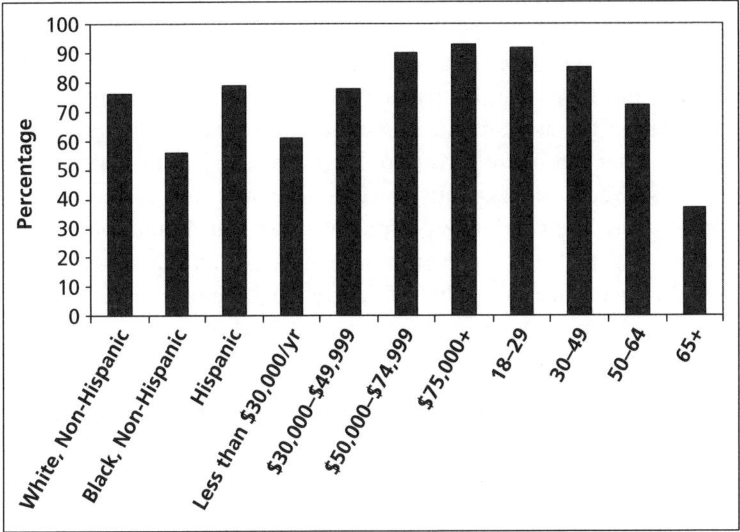

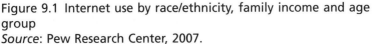

Figure 9.1 Internet use by race/ethnicity, family income and age group
Source: Pew Research Center, 2007.

performance in online assessment programs, to the extent that less advantaged groups are less familiar and comfortable with technology. Although some research suggests that minorities tend to view technology-based selection processes positively regardless of where they access them from,[12] there is little research addressing whether differences in access rates could have an appreciable impact on the resulting scores. Therefore, it would be prudent to consider potential differences in familiarity and access to technology when implementing online staffing systems, especially for jobs where many applicants may not have easy access to the Internet. For some programs, offering assessment orientation and alternative testing facilities for those with no home access may be helpful.

The Candidate Experience

Job candidate perceptions and reactions to the testing process are an important component of the recruitment process. Any of the issues mentioned above could create a negative experience for the candidate, which may result in a range of potentially undesirable consequences. Your corporate image and brand may suffer, candidates in certain groups may be discouraged from participating in the process, and those that do participate may not perform up to their potential on the assessment. As we mentioned earlier, there is some evidence that candidate perception of testing conditions is associated with assessment scores. Thus, paying close attention to the staffing process from the candidate perspective is an important component of planning for the implementation of your staffing system. This includes ensuring appropriate content, a reliable and easy-to-navigate delivery system, and good environmental conditions.

Strategies for Managing Online Assessment Systems

Given the imposing array of potential problems that may arise with online test administration, what can you do to minimize the effects upon your talent assessment program? A number of strategies for managing testing conditions may be adopted to safeguard against these various threats to the quality of measurement and integrity of the system. A key component worth highlighting is to continuously monitor testing operations and identify opportunities for improvement. Gathering feedback from candidates immediately following the online assessment is one approach. It is also helpful to review test proctor reports and help-desk logs to identify trends and needed process improvements. Monitoring assessment results to ensure that problematic administration sites are not affecting test scores, candidate flow, and recruitment is critical. Examples of specific strategies that may be considered to address environmental issues and concerns are outlined in the following chart.

Summary

In this chapter, we have explored key environmental issues and potential pitfalls that could undermine your online staffing program if left unattended. The importance of environmental quality control cannot be overstated. While no system is perfect, the most successful programs are founded upon operational standards, appropriate facilities and technology, and careful oversight of delivery. When it comes to planning, executing, and managing your staffing system, administration conditions are an essential consideration.

Strategies for Managing Online Assessment.

Issues and Concerns	*Strategies*
Cheating	• *Authentication:* obtain identifying information about the examinee, preferably verified before enabling access; unfiltered access should not be allowed. • *Controlled access:* give single access to known candidate with limited time availability. • *Warnings:* publish warning to candidates regarding verification or follow-up assessment, and consequences of cheating or breeching security. • *Security agreement:* require candidates to agree to conform with security and anti-cheating provisions. • *Timed administration:* use timed tests to limit the ways in which examinees can cheat. • *Item banking:* rotate test content in parallel forms to minimize item (question) exposure and opportunity to cheat. • *Follow-up assessment:* conduct a second stage assessment of candidates who pass an unproctored test. • *Multi-mode convergence:* compare scores on alternative measures of the same skill or attribute; look for agreement, within the precision of measurement.
Nonstandard environmental conditions	• *User guidelines:* provide guidelines for preparing the test environment and for administering the test. • *Monitor the environment:* survey candidates, proctors, clients of the process. • *Monitor help desk calls:* analyze data for trends to derive operational improvements.

Continued

Issues and Concerns	*Strategies*
Technology issues	• *Architecture:* system design should enable consistency across a range of hardware, software, and connectivity configurations. • *Presentation:* preserve test content appearance, placement, and accessibility. • *Navigation:* enable examinees to answer questions and advance similar to paper-based tests. • *System guidelines:* provide requirements and specifications for local systems and tips for configuration and use. • *Technical support:* ensure that support is available for users.
Test security	• Web-based delivery in *"kiosk" mode* (locked browser) • Present tests in *full-screen mode*, in a standardized format • *Prevent access* to the test items • *Disable use of system commands* during the test • *Limit unnecessary navigation* • *Encrypt data transmission* • *Password-protected logins* • *Key-based test sessions with expiration* • *Web patrol:* routinely search for sites offering test information
Unqualified applicants	• *Application self assessment and pre-screen:* establish basic qualifications • *Realistic job previews:* help pre-qualify the candidate pool by encouraging self-selection • *Control access:* avoid open unfiltered access to assessment content

Continued

Issues and Concerns	*Strategies*
Demographic differences in Access	• *Provide alternative testing locations:* monitor group use and make alternatives available for examinees who lack adequate local facilities • *Practice test and tutorial:* provide orientation and practice using the online system
Candidate acceptance	• *Candidate orientation resources:* publicize exam procedures and alternatives

Chapter 10

Cross-Cultural Deployment

Internet-based systems enable organizations to operate their staffing processes on a global basis. Once business processes are converted to web delivery, companies large and small can just as easily deploy online systems across town, the nation, or the world. Technology-wise this may be true; however, a key challenge is raised when organizations implement staffing procedures across cultures and languages. As businesses extend their reach into global consumer and labor markets, there is increasingly strong demand for multilingual assessment programs to acquire the best talent to support business processes wherever they may be needed. The Internet provides an efficient means to recruit and assess candidates worldwide, offering businesses the opportunity to standardize and leverage their talent management processes. However, good technology is not enough to transport processes across cultures.

More food for thought: Even domestic talent programs may be considered to be global in the sense that candidate pools are becoming increasingly diverse and multilingual. It seems that the demand for cross-cultural talent assessment has reached a tipping point in domestic staffing operations. In the United States, for example, the need for staffing programs to address multilingual labor pools has increased substantially. The number of Spanish speakers, in particular, increased dramatically in the United States over the two decades between 1980 and 2000, from 10.2 to 24.7 million people (an increase of 242%).[1] It is estimated that 46% of the approximately 25 million Hispanic adults in the United States are bilingual Spanish–English

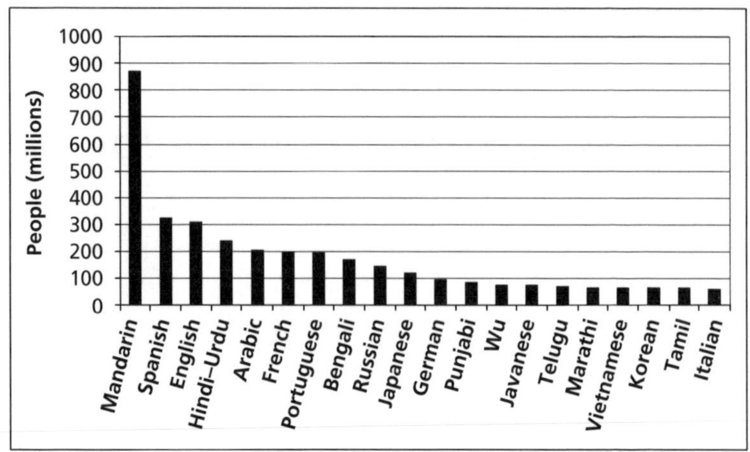

Figure 10.1 The twenty most common spoken languages

speakers.[2] Also interesting to note is that Spanish has surpassed English in worldwide use and is now the second most commonly spoken language in the world, following Mandarin Chinese. The top twenty world languages are listed in Figure 10.1.[3]

The globalization of business, increasing diversity within labor markets, and the continued quest for talent combine to heighten the need for cross-cultural talent acquisition and management programs. This poses a dilemma: *How can you deploy talent assessment procedures across cultures in a manner that preserves standards and relevance?* In this chapter, we review key issues that arise when implementing talent assessment procedures across cultures. As we do, please keep in mind that although the term "culture" can be defined in different ways, we use it here to represent the broad set of customs, conventions, language, and beliefs that are predominant in a region.

Adapting Talent Assessment Programs across Cultures

Whether you are deploying a global talent assessment program or a domestic program with a highly diverse candidate pool, you are faced with the challenge of ensuring that your business processes are effective across different cultures and languages. There are a variety of scenarios where cross-cultural deployment of talent assessment comes into play. Examples of three scenarios are outlined below.

- *Bilingual and native speakers assessed in the same market:* Under this scenario, bilingual candidates are assessed in a language other than their primary language. A number of factors will typically drive this scenario, such as: the labor market – the availability of qualified candidates and their lingual proficiency; language requirements for the job; and the degree to which different organizational units operate interdependently. For example, it is quite common in U.S. labor markets to encounter job candidates for whom English is a second language (ESL). It is also common for global companies to employ bilingual English speakers, so that business processes can be deployed in the same language in remote locations that interact frequently. For many years, employers operated under the assumption that if English is required for the job, the assessment program could be implemented "as is" in English. However, this approach can result in employers overlooking talented candidates, leading some to develop strategies to recruit and select bilingual employees. To this end, employers in strong multilingual labor markets have translated portions of the recruitment and selection assessment program into multiple languages, while including a language proficiency assessment component to ensure adequate fluency in the core language requirements for the job.
- *Native speakers assessed in separate markets:* Under this scenario, the staffing program is adapted to the native culture and language of each location of a business operation. This scenario is common for organizations with multinational locations that operate independently and where there is a predominant language required. For example, a global company with offices in the United States, Europe, and Asia adapts its talent assessment program to the unique requirements of each county, translating materials into different languages and modifying certain components to reflect local customs and conventions. For the most part, each country's talent program operates separately, although efforts are made to retain the corporate brand and business standards.
- *Global talent program – bilingual and native assessment in multiple markets:* This scenario is more complex, blending features of the first two. Many variations are possible. An example would be a

U.S. company with European offices, where the talent assessment program developed and implemented at HQ is adapted to the primary language for each European satellite office. Within many of the locations, bilingual candidates comprise a substantial portion of the labor pool, causing recruiters to push for adapting portions of the selection assessment program into additional languages to accommodate bilingual candidates' needs, with the aim of increasing the qualified talent pool.

Issues and Challenges

Implementing talent assessment programs across cultures requires careful consideration of a number of factors and potential pitfalls that can affect the success of your program. Generally speaking, these include administrative, measurement, professional, and technology issues.

Administrative Considerations

When considering whether to give assessments that cross cultural groups, several factors should be examined, including the language requirements for the work, the proficiency level required, and rules for case-by-case implementation. Each of these considerations is briefly elaborated below.

Language requirements. As we discussed earlier in Chapter 6, a fundamental step in talent management is to identify the knowledge, skills, abilities, and other characteristics (KSAOs) required for job success. This includes determining language requirements for the job and aligning the selection assessment program with job requirements. Determining the language needs for a job is a straightforward process in most respects, and can be accomplished by addressing several basic questions about language use and requirements within the organization, as well as with customers and partners. These questions include:

- What is the primary operating language of the business?
- What communication modes are required (reading, writing, listening, speaking)?

- What level of language proficiency is required?
- Under what circumstances, if any, can alternative languages be used?

In some circumstances, employers may have flexibility in job design to allow for alternative languages to be used. For example, it may be acceptable for certain manufacturing and warehouse jobs if a candidate can speak fluently in the desired primary operating language of the company, while little or no fluency in writing may be required. In other instances, proficiency in all modes of the primary operating language of the company may be essential. For example, with an inside sales job at a call center, it is essential that candidates be proficient in written and oral communication.

Language proficiency. A key issue is how language proficiency will be determined. A common approach is for candidates to self-assess their capabilities to communicate in a target language. For example, using

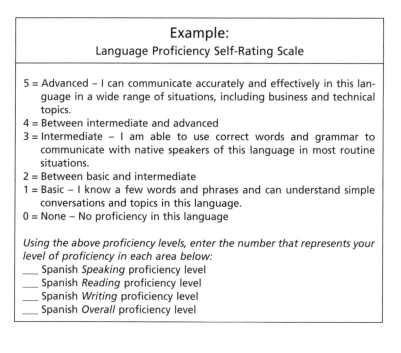

Example:

Language Proficiency Self-Rating Scale

5 = Advanced – I can communicate accurately and effectively in this language in a wide range of situations, including business and technical topics.
4 = Between intermediate and advanced
3 = Intermediate – I am able to use correct words and grammar to communicate with native speakers of this language in most routine situations.
2 = Between basic and intermediate
1 = Basic – I know a few words and phrases and can understand simple conversations and topics in this language.
0 = None – No proficiency in this language

Using the above proficiency levels, enter the number that represents your level of proficiency in each area below:
___ Spanish *Speaking* proficiency level
___ Spanish *Reading* proficiency level
___ Spanish *Writing* proficiency level
___ Spanish *Overall* proficiency level

a numeric rating scale such as the one shown in the box below, candidates may be asked to evaluate their proficiency in the target language. These types of ratings have been found to be reasonably effective in predicting a candidate's actual proficiency on a language skills test.[4] The American Council on the Teaching of Foreign Languages (ACTFL) is a good resource for defining language proficiency standards.[5]

Of course, a more direct method of determining language proficiency is to use an assessment of language skills (e.g., reading comprehension, writing skills, and vocabulary). Language proficiency assessment tools are available from a variety of publishers.

In some settings, it may be feasible to allow candidates to complete an assessment in their native language and use a separate assessment of proficiency in the target language. For example, a selection assessment comprised of a problem-solving test and a personality assessment may be delivered in Spanish, and a separate assessment of English proficiency may be administered to ensure basic fluency needed for certain business operations.

Implementation. One of the pitfalls in cross-cultural staffing programs is the potential confusion among administrators in knowing when and how to offer candidates assessments in alternative languages. It is important to establish clear policies and processes for identifying candidates' primary language and their proficiency in the operating language of the company. It is also important that when assessments are available in alternative languages, candidates are provided a reasonable and discreet means to opt for them. For example, one effective approach is to allow candidates to self-evaluate their level of language proficiency and be offered a choice of assessment languages prior to the testing session, contingent upon their self-appraised skill level.

Measurement Quality Concerns

A key concern in cross-cultural assessment is that measurement of candidate attributes remains accurate, valid, and unaffected by the adaptation of the assessment from one language and culture to another. This is conceptually similar to the concerns raised in Chapter 9 about the possibility of extraneous environmental factors affecting measurement quality. To the extent that cultural differences in the interpretation of assessment questions differ, "noise" is added to the information obtained. This means that scores are less likely to reflect real candidate differences on the attribute of interest. We want to ensure that language and cultural translation does not change the nature of what is measured by the assessment tool, and at the same time, is comparable in meaning and difficulty across cultures. To this end, practitioners must be aware of potential problems that can arise when translating assessment tools.

Adapting assessments for cross-cultural use. A variety of concerns emerge in adapting assessment procedures across cultures. These are outlined below in the context of typical steps that would be followed in translating an assessment:

- *Specification:* Guidelines are needed for the translator to understand key features of the assessment tool to ensure they are not altered in the translation. The intended KSAO to be measured and factors that affect the difficulty of the test questions should be preserved in the translation.
- *Content conversion:* Working with a professional language translation service will help to ensure that proper conventions are followed. A useful resource for translation services and standards is the American Translators Association website.[6] Translators may start by completing a literal translation and then perform a contextual adaptation in instances where it is necessary to identify an equivalent concept that may be expressed differently in another culture. Language rules, conventions, phrasing, and cultural metaphors and concepts (idiom) are not universal and, therefore, judgment is often required on the part of the translator to express comparable concepts correctly and in manner that appears natural. For example, phrases such as "spend time," "fall into place," or "easy-going" may not translate well, if at all, into other languages and cultures. During the contextual review, it is important to consider different dialects or "regionalisms" to ensure that the language is acceptable and understandable to a

wide audience. As a double check on the accuracy of the process, it is common to conduct a back-translation of the translated document into the original language. To be effective, back-translation should be done by a different translator than the original translation; the two first-language versions should then be compared for congruence. This process can become complex and requires special subject matter expertise when the translation requires contextual interpretation and substitution of concepts or scenarios.

- *Expert review:* Individual translators may not completely capture all that is needed in an assessment translation. To ensure that the translation will apply to the target market and strike the right balance of localization, it is helpful to conduct focus group sessions with bilingual people representing major regionalisms of the original and new language to ensure that the translated version is understandable, of comparable difficulty, and preserves the context across various language conventions. An example set of expert review guidelines is shown in the box below.
- *Data collection and analysis:* Problems with translated assessment questions may not be readily apparent and can emerge when administered under real stakes conditions. It is usually helpful to administer the translated assessment to bilingual and native speakers on a pilot basis and then analyze the statistical properties of the questions and test scores to ensure that their score distributions and other statistical properties are reasonable. The results can be helpful in a number of ways. You may find that certain test questions have become too difficult or too easy, for a variety of reasons related to the translation (e.g., the translated text is at a higher or lower level of reading difficulty; differences between multiple-choice response options have become confusing, or at the other extreme, the translation provides clues to the correct answer or makes it easy to eliminate incorrect answers). You can use this information to refine the translation to better approximate the intended difficulty level. Another possible finding is that cross-cultural differences between candidate pools (e.g., education, language proficiency) may lead to score differences, suggesting that culturally specific test norms would be useful (e.g., for programs operating in different countries).

Example:
Review Guidelines

- The terms, phrasing, and examples used in the translated version are meaningful and commonly understood in the culture.
- The translated test version does not contain language that might be considered offensive in the culture.
- Each translated question requires the test taker to perform substantially the same task as the original question. Make sure the process or strategy used to determine the correct answer in the translated version is the same as that used in the original version.
- Each translated question is the same difficulty level as the original question. For example, check to see that:
  - there are not fewer ways to derive an answer in the translated questions than in the original questions;
  - the translated questions do not make any of the answers more obvious.

Equivalence in measurement. An important and complex issue in multilingual talent assessment programs is whether assessment scores obtained for a version in one language are equivalent to a version in another language. The term "equivalence" means that we are measuring the same thing in comparable units. For example, a measure of Conscientiousness reflects the same characteristic in Mandarin and English, and a score at the 70th percentile on one form is comparable to the 70th percentile on the other and can be used interchangeably.

As it turns out, establishing equivalence of translated assessments can be a complex process, and there are a variety of approaches to conducting the necessary R&D studies.[7] In general these entail administering the translated and original assessment forms to different samples of bilingual and/or native language speakers, and analyzing the properties of the tests and their interrelationships. These data are also useful to establish norms and cut scores for the assessments.

An especially complicating factor in cross-cultural studies is that people vary in their levels of multilingual proficiency and this can impact performance on both the original and translated forms of the assessment.[8] For example, it has been found that bilingual proficiency differences can impact the results of test equivalence studies, making translated forms appear to be less comparable unless adjustments are made for this effect. A further complicating factor is that people's educational differences seem to interact with their language proficiency, so you need to be careful to control for educational differences before making conclusions about the equivalence between measures.

Assessment type and cultural considerations. Some types of assessments will translate more easily than others. As a general rule, the more verbal content and colloquial expressions that are included in an assessment, the more likely it is that adaptation will require a contextual translation. For example, personality and attitude tests typically require translators to search for equivalent concepts that may not directly translate from one culture to another. Case in point: in the United States, questions about being competitive and winning are often taken to represent individual achievement, while this concept may not be socially acceptable in a team-oriented Asian culture. On the other hand, an assessment of math skills is relatively easy to translate across cultures. For this reason, multi-cultural assessment programs often utilize non-verbal measures (e.g., symbolic reasoning in lieu of verbal reasoning).

Professional Challenges

In Chapter 3 we reviewed professional standards and principles for measurement and personnel selection, including the *Standards for Educational and Psychological Testing* and the *Principles for the Validation and Use of Personnel Selection Procedures.* In addition to these, the International Testing Commission publishes the more comprehensive *ITC Guidelines on Adapting Tests.*[9] Together these best-practices documents include considerable discussion of technical requirements and considerations for translating and adapting assessments. The principal focus of these standards is upon measurement quality and equivalence of adapted and original measures across candidate pools. In practice, it may be difficult to achieve all of the suggested standards; however, it is advisable to choose assessment tools that adhere to as many of the standards as possible, and to implement adapted tools with these standards in mind. An outline of relevant assessment standards is provided in the box below.

Cross-Cultural Testing Standards Summary

Standards for Educational and Psychological Testing
- Reliability and validity should be established for translated tests; evidence of comparability should be reported.

Principles for the Validation and Use of Personnel Selection Procedures
- Global selection systems should consider locally accepted practices.

ITC Guidelines on Adapting Tests
- Adaptation process should account for cultural differences in target markets.
- Test content and methods should be familiar to target markets.
- Appropriate research and statistical techniques should be applied to establish the equivalence of the language versions of the test.
- Score differences among samples should not be taken at face value; further work is required to understand them.
- Expert judgments should be compiled to improve adaptation accuracy.

Technology Challenges

Another significant consideration in the cross-cultural deployment of talent assessment tools is the adaptation of the software systems that deliver them. In addition to the assessment content, the user interface with online assessment systems must also be adapted and translated when these systems are intended to operate across cultures. These system interface components include:

- Candidate touch-points in the system, including login screens, tutorials, instructions, navigation bars and buttons, and pop-up messages that might occur during the assessment session (e.g., "*Are you sure you are finished?*").
- Administrator functions such as account set-up screens, assessment configuration utilities, product ordering tools, and screens for managing test "keys" and sessions. Depending upon the scope of your online staffing program, administrative users may be proficient in the system base language (e.g., English), so that translation of administrative functions may not be required.
- End-user functions, such as accessing, viewing, and printing candidate score reports; also, functions for generating account summary and activity reports.

From a systems design standpoint, cross-cultural deployment of online assessments requires special functionality to be included, such as: methods for cataloging and launching alternative language versions of the same assessment tool; configuring the language options for administrators, candidates, and end-users who may require the same or different languages; and expanded database capabilities to capture additional labels and text associated with the language of the assessment tool. The assessment system must be designed to accommodate these types of functions such that delivery of the translated assessment content fits seamlessly with the translated user interface. It is important to prepare for the resource and time requirements associated with this effort, and to ensure that adequate functionality exists to support your multilingual assessment program.

Finally, there are important system administration considerations related to online deployment across cultures. One is establishing business rules for when alternative language assessments should be used and who is authorized to decide when to use them. These business rules can be enforced programmatically with defined user roles that are limited to certain system accounts that are enabled to select the assessment language. Another consideration is the provision for technical user support in the languages and regions where the assessment will be used. Depending upon the volume and geographic breadth of your talent assessment program, alternative approaches could include: using a central single-language technical support center supported by on-demand telephone translation services; establishing regional technical support centers in the native cultures; or working with a call center outsourcing firm to provide extended high-volume, multilingual support.

Strategies for Cross-Cultural Deployment

Worldwide availability of talent systems requires careful design and application when cross-cultural deployment is introduced. Many of the concerns and best practices described in other chapters apply here as well – focus on good measurement, standardization, and consistent processes. Key strategies for deploying cross-cultural assessments include:

- Determine job language requirements: consider business requirements and allowable alternatives.
- Understand the labor market: what are the predominant languages?
- Use assessments that are well suited for translation and multicultural application.
- Use professionally translated tools: there are many nuances to translation that an untrained eye will not catch.
- Localize content when possible: conduct focus group reviews to ensure that translated content applies to regionalisms of the language.
- Delivery software requires translation too: user interfaces must also be translated and adapted as an integral part of the assessment.
- Gather normative data: benchmark translated assessments to your labor market to provide a framework for interpreting scores in different markets.
- Design sensible administrative processes: ensure that the carefully designed assessment system is used consistently and appropriately.

Summary

As we learned in this chapter, great technology and systems are not enough to transport talent assessment programs across cultures. Cross-cultural assessment raises some complex issues, which if addressed, can help assure the successful deployment of your staffing system in today's diverse talent markets. Careful attention must be paid to adapting assessments to target markets in such a way that the quality of measurement information is preserved and wise staffing decisions can be made in any language.

Chapter 11

Candidate Privacy and Data Security

Another set of issues raised by the use of online HR tools relates to the security of the information that is generated and the privacy considerations of the individuals who contribute that information. These issues have a common thread: they both involve issues of data protection. Data security generally involves the protection of private and/or sensitive information against unintentional loss or distribution; privacy considerations extend beyond security to include intentional distribution of candidate information. Because of the rapid expansion of electronic platforms that hold personal information, data security and privacy protection are rapidly expanding topics within software engineering, HR practice, and law.

This chapter focuses on the major issues that must be addressed when designing and implementing HR tools that collect and retain personal data. Generally, both the providers of online tools and the organizations that use them are responsible for ensuring that data privacy and security are maintained. The emphasis here is on the system elements and functions that should be available within online systems in order to maintain candidate privacy and data security.

The reasons for careful attention to this topic should be obvious: online processes can generate risk for organizations in several ways that are associated with data protection. For example, the damage to operational processes due to the loss of critical data, reputation, and liability due to personal damage are among the concerns organizations may face. Individuals also face risks associated with undesired solicitation, abuse of financial information, and even identity theft that could result from improper treatment of their personal data. These risks are magnified by a growing network of regulations that address the proper treatment of personal information. Organizations may be exposed to liabilities and risks if they construct their online systems in a manner that does not comply. European regulations are especially important for organizations to understand, because they provide a well-developed benchmark, and also because organizations around the world must abide by them if they collect data from citizens of the European Union. In fact, guidelines for organizations based in the United States have been developed to closely mirror the European framework.[1]

European Data Protection Rules: A Foundational Framework

As the use of online processes for recruitment and selection extends the reach of these tools to a worldwide audience, organizations must be aware of, and compliant with, the various international rules that apply to the transfer of individual data across political borders. Of primary importance are the European data protection regulations.

Internet-based tools that allow, for example, job seekers in Europe to apply for a job using systems that are hosted on computers located in the United States are by design collecting personal data and transferring these data across borders. By engaging in this activity an organization in the United States could potentially be in violation of the domestic laws of the European Union (EU) Member States. These laws were implemented as a result of the EU Directive on Data Protection that aims to prohibit the free flow of personal information from EU nations to countries that had been deemed to have "inadequate" privacy protection regulations, such as the United States at the time.

The Directive, which went into effect in 1998, underscores the difference between both the cultures and legal systems of Europe and the United States. In Europe, privacy protection is viewed as a personal right. To protect this right, the various EU member countries have enacted a network of legislation, administered through government data protection agencies. The Directive's primary intended purpose is to set minimum privacy protection standards for each of the EU member countries to facilitate the transfer of personal data within the EU. In the United States, by contrast, the protection of private information is viewed less uniformly, with differing standards for varying circumstances. For example, there are separate regulations for healthcare and financial data. Therefore, privacy protection in the United States is guided only by limited legislation and regulation.

Organizations that use Internet-based HR systems that could be used by Europeans have several compliance options. Two approaches are most common: first, organizations can seek permission from data providers (i.e., job seekers) regarding exactly how and where their data will be processed. Second, organizations may join a U.S. Department of Commerce program that certifies them as a safe harbor for personal data. This certification is based on the organization's willingness to declare their adherence to seven Safe Harbor Privacy Principles, which the Commerce Department negotiated with the EU. The seven principles are shown in the box below.[2]

Good to Know:

Seven Principles of Privacy Protection

1. *Notice.* Individuals must be informed, as early as possible and in unambiguous language, about the organization's reasons for collecting and using their personal information.
2. *Choice.* Individuals must be allowed to decide if and how their information is to be used or disclosed to third parties beyond the purpose originally specified and authorized by the organization collecting the information.
3. *Onward transfer.* Personal information may only be transferred to a third party when the data provider has been given both notice and choice about the data transfer. One organization can transfer data to another without participant assent only if the third-party organization also is qualified as a safe harbor or otherwise satisfies the requirements of the EU Directive.
4. *Access.* Within logistical reason, individuals must have access to and be able to correct, add to, or delete their personal information where it is deemed inaccurate.
5. *Security.* Data must be reasonably protected from loss, misuse, unauthorized access and disclosure.
6. *Data integrity.* Personal information must be relevant, reliable, accurate, current, complete, and used only for the purpose for which it was collected and authorized by the individual.
7. *Enforcement.* Organizations must provide mechanisms for complaints and recourse, procedures for verifying adherence to the safe harbor principles and obligations to remedy problems.

HR professionals who are involved with the implementation of IT systems that are to hold personal or sensitive data should consider how these systems' features and functions support compliance with the data protection principles. Failure to comply could result in fines and other liabilities for both employers and vendors of automated systems. The major considerations are discussed for each principle in the following section.

Design Considerations for Data and Privacy Protection

Notice

The key issue under this principle is whether the participants in the process (e.g., job seekers) are presented with information early in the process that allows them to understand how the information they are about to provide will be used by the organization. This principle also implies that *all* uses of the information are described, not just the immediate purpose. Organizations must then abide by these uses of the data.

For example, an organization may intend to use a job seeker's profile in two ways: First, a personal profile may be collected for a selection process that is associated with a specific job for which the job seeker expressed interest. Second, if the job seeker is not selected for the initial role, the information will be stored for comparison against the requirements for future roles for which the job seeker might be qualified. The job seeker may then be contacted to inquire about potential interest in the second role. In this example, the job seekers must be provided with adequate notice that their data will be treated this way before providing the information for the initial job. All purposes and uses of the data should be clear to the participants in an online process before they are asked to provide any personal information.

Pre-configured online tools should allow the organization to customize the text that the website user sees before they provide any personal data. Unless this text clearly describes the purposes for which the data will be used, the organization (not the online tool provider) could face liabilities related to improper notice.

What is *Personal* and *Sensitive* Information?

Personal information is any information that identifies a specific living person, such as a name, address, telephone number, or e-mail address.

Sensitive information includes data regarding race or ethnic origin as well as health, legal, or political information.

HR data collected during the selection process may contain both personal and sensitive information because race is often collected during the application process.

Choice

In situations where the organization may desire to use personal information for purposes other than those described in the original notice, it is critical that the participant actively chooses to have the information used in this new manner. This requirement essentially reestablishes the principle of "notice" for the new purpose, since the participant must be informed about the new purpose when they are given a choice to participate.

In the example above, after the initial job seeker profile is collected, if the organization later decides to use the profile information to select some participants for special marketing activities related to their product, the individuals would need to be notified about this use of their data and provide permission to use the information for this purpose. So, as new purposes for the data emerge, the participants should be re-contacted for their permission to use the information for the new purposes.

Onward Transfer

If an organization desires to provide personal information to a third party, they must provide both notice and choice regarding this transfer of the data. Under this requirement, one organization can transfer data to another without participant assent if the purpose of the transfer is consistent with the original purpose of the data collection *and* if the third-party organization also qualifies as a safe harbor or otherwise satisfies the requirements of the EU Directive.

In the context of online recruitment and selection, onward transfer of personal data occurs when information collected in one part of the selection process is provided to a third party so that they can conduct another part of the process. For example, personal information that is collected when job seekers first apply for a role may be transferred to a third party for the purpose of conducting a background check as a part of that same selection process. If the background check provider only uses the information for this purpose and abides by the data protection principles, then this transfer is allowable under the Safe Harbor Principles. Organizations should also describe any data transfer to the job seeker before they are asked to submit personal information; that way the Notice and Choice principles are covered and the transfer will be consistent with the agreed-upon purpose of the data submission. Again, this requirement can be achieved via text that is used to describe the purpose of the data collection to job seekers (see the box at the end of this section for an example). Upon reviewing this information, if the job seeker decides they do not want their information used in the manner that is described, they should be able to exit from the process without their data being stored for use within the system.

Access

Another system feature that is critical for proper data handling is the facility for job seekers to keep critical information up to date. This condition typically applies to information such as name, contact information, and other descriptive information. However, if the process includes questions about background (such as prior jobs or work experiences) that could become inaccurate as time passes, job seekers should ideally be able to change this information also.

The Access principle should be considered carefully in conjunction with other system goals when making determinations about what information to allow job seekers to change once they have submitted it for review. Some information, such as the job seeker's responses to assessment questions, should not be changed after submission because these changes may compromise the security and integrity of the assessment itself. Therefore, most systems allow changes only to the personal background and contact information sections of the process. Many systems also allow job seekers to request that their data profile be deleted from the system if they no longer wish to be considered for employment.

Security

Without proper data security, the privacy of personal data cannot be assured. So data security is an important underpinning of the data protection regulations. System providers should take reasonable precautions against unauthorized users from gaining access to personal data. While the technical aspects of Internet security extend beyond the scope of this book, a general introduction to the topic is provided in the next section of this chapter.

Data Integrity

The Integrity principle draws from the other principles and extends them to emphasize that personal information must be relevant, reliable, accurate, current, complete, and used only for the purpose for which it was collected and authorized by the individual. This principle raises the obligation to ensure that the data used to inform important decisions are in the proper condition to support that purpose. In addition to the protections discussed above, organizations should ensure that the databases they maintain are free from common problems such as data corruption, formatting errors, or misuse by poorly trained operators. The principle additionally demands that the users of personal information take steps to ensure the currency of the information that has been collected. This can be achieved through careful attention to the Access principle, and also by setting "expiration" dates for assessment data that may lose its accuracy and predictive capability over time. These intervals should be determined in consultation with the developers of the assessment tools that are used in the process.

Enforcement

The final principle indicates that when setting up online systems, you must provide a process for the participants to register complaints and for providing solutions to privacy and data protection issues.

Additionally, you are obligated to develop procedures for verifying that your process complies with the Safe Harbor Principles.

Several organizations have been established to help companies comply with the various privacy and data protection rules. Services such as TRUSTe and BBBOnline will review data privacy policies and procedures in light of the applicable rules and will act as arbiters to settle disputes over data handing, thereby satisfying the Enforcement principle.

Other Privacy Rules

In addition to the EU rules, a growing number of U.S. laws deal with privacy considerations. For example, California laws have also been enacted that require a privacy statement to be posted on any site that collects personal information from California residents, and additional rules require the disclosure of any breach of personal data security.

Case law will also emerge over time to distinguish acceptable practices from the unacceptable ones. Consider the case of now the defunct online toy seller Toysmart,[3] which sold customer information despite its vow, published on its site, never to do so. This case, and surely others to follow, should serve as a reminder that you will be held accountable for the policies that are published on your website.

Clearly, the liabilities associated with these responsibilities need to be carefully examined with respect to any HR processes, and online recruitment and selection processes are of particular concern due to their broad reach to the public at large. When you use online recruitment and selection processes you should be aware of these privacy considerations and take steps to ensure that your online tools are compliant; otherwise, Internet-based systems that collect information broadly from job seekers will raise risks associated with liabilities under both EU and U.S. laws.

Fundamentals of Internet Data Security

In addition to the system features that allow you to collect and manage data in a manner that protects individual privacy, there are system features that enhance data integrity and security that should be con-

Example:
Participant Agreement Text

Before you begin the application process, read the agreement below and indicate whether you accept or do not accept each of the terms.

The data that you provide will be stored outside the European Union for a limited period of time. However, in processing and storing the data you give us, we will comply with the European Union Directive on data protection and privacy and the Data Protection Act 1998, which implements that Directive.

The data will be used solely by XYZ Corporation or its affiliates and will not be divulged to any third party, unless otherwise required by legal requirement or order.

In the event that you would like us to amend or remove your data from our database please contact our security officer at Security.Officer@XYZcorp.Com. For more information on these data processing, storage and protection policies, please review the *XYZ Privacy Statement*.

Terms:

I acknowledge that the information I will provide is correct to the best of my knowledge and I understand that any inaccurate information could lead to a retraction of employment offer or dismissal if employment has taken place. I further acknowledge that I am completing this application on my own behalf. I understand the above and consent to my personal data being stored in a non-European Union country.

Do you accept the terms set forth in this agreement?
□ I accept the terms set forth in this agreement.
□ I do not accept the terms of this agreement. (This will end your online assessment.)

sidered as you implement any online tool that contains personal or sensitive data. Internet security is a rapidly evolving area, and if you are implementing online tools, you should collaborate with an IT professional that has specific knowledge of the latest standards and practices. The following discussion provides some of the basic concepts and techniques for enhancing data security. Your online systems provider should be well versed on the appropriate security components for the systems they support.

Generally considered, information security has three objectives: confidentiality, integrity, and availability.[4] That is, in order to maintain security, systems should enable data to be viewed by authorized users, changed by authorized users, and available for the business purposes they are intended to support. There are several system components that support these objectives that you should examine when considering the security of online systems.[5] A few common components are described below.

Password Protection

All system users should be required to use a password to gain entry into the software; the only exception should be job seekers who first enter the system from a career portal; in this case, once the job seeker is asked to provide personal information, a password should be generated or self-created to allow the individual to return to the system, if appropriate. Secure passwords should not be common dictionary words, as these can be easily hacked. Ideally, passwords are a combination of letters and numbers and are at least eight characters long. Other forms of user authentication are also increasingly common; however, they are rarely applied to HR data. For example, biometrics such as fingerprints are becoming more common in systems with heightened security requirements.

Role-Based Security

Access to various system elements and data files should be restricted based on the identity of the individual user and his or her role as a system user. Role-based security features allow for the presentation of only the portions of the system that a particular user is allowed to access. These protections may also restrict the operations that are allowable by each role or user type: some users may have read-only rights, others may have read and write privileges, while a third group is also able to delete entire records.

For example, job seekers should only have access to the information within their individual data record and the elements of the system that allow them to explore job opportunities and to apply for jobs. Recruiters may have access to the pool of candidates that pertain to the openings for which they are responsible, but not to those in other regions or divisions. Hiring managers, similarly, may be constrained so they only see the candidates that are relevant for their job opening. System administrators may have broad rights that allow them to access to all system components, including features that allow them to assign system rights to other users. Additionally, recruiters and managers may not have rights to change candidate data, while candidates and system administrators may have this right.

Ideally, online recruiting and selection tools should allow for the creation of user roles in a manner that is consistent with their operations and business needs. One-size-fits-all roles seldom work in complex organizations, so you should pay careful attention to the allowable flexibilities in this area, lest you find yourself having to create new organizational processes to accommodate rigid system roles.

History and Log Files

Also critical for ensuring data integrity are features that track access and changes to the database records. These tools typically log the date, time, and user who accessed a particular record, and the change that was made. This information can be critical for tracking unauthorized changes, but also can be important for reinstating prior entries, when inappropriate changes are made. Some government audit requirements, such as those described by the OFCCP's Internet applicant rules, entail the re-creation of search results when these database searches result in the selection of job seekers into an applicant pool. History files can also be used for storing these search commands to meet these requirements.

Encryption

Various methods are available for encrypting sensitive data as it flows between systems. Many applicants will not provide personal information unless they are provided with secure site access that prevents malicious interlopers from intercepting the communication between a data provider and the server. Tools such as Secure Socket Layer (SSL) protocol make these transactions private because the information is encoded such that only the two systems involved in the transaction have the key to unlock the code. If data are to be available outside of a central system (for example, downloaded onto a laptop), it is also advisable to use forms of encoding that will protect the information from users that do not possess a key that authorizes access to the information. Even if full data encryption is not available, scrambling or eliminating highly sensitive data such social security numbers is advisable. Note the experience of the Gap, Inc., where a laptop was stolen that contained records on 800,000 job applicants, and some of the information lost included applicants' social security numbers.[6]

Additional Security Considerations

Of course, many essential elements of strong data protection are not software features, but rather entail issues of hardware configuration, physical security of your software provider's data center, and the policies and procedures that govern proper data access, usage, and maintenance. Well-run systems should have written policies and defined organizational roles that focus on data protection.

As you consider the implementation of online staffing tools we recommend that the components and processes we have described in this chapter be supplemented with the knowledge of an experienced IT security specialist. These professionals typically have well defined audit procedures, such as those listed in the box below, for evaluating the data protection practices for the online systems you are considering.

Typical Areas Covered in a Security Audit

- Physical characteristics of the data center (location, physical security, surveillance, temperature/environmental controls, fire protection, etc.)
- Network architecture, including server configurations and firewalls
- Hardware and transmission line descriptions
- Operating systems and database languages
- Tested volume levels for maximum simultaneous users
- Data security and encryption processes
- Disaster recover plans and up-time history
- System access controls and user account management
- User support services
- System monitoring processes for performance, intrusion, and viruses
- Research & development and quality assurance processes
- Security policies, procedures, and training
- Employee background checks and security clearances

Chapter 12

Conclusion: The (Possible) Future of Automated Staffing

In this book, we have reviewed many of the options and issues that are faced when designing and implementing systems for staffing organizations. We have focused on tools that are now relatively common in organizations with large staffing needs. Several major themes and trends are evident in this overview: the dramatic impact of technology in transforming staffing processes, the pressure to integrate adjacent or complementary components of the staffing process, increased globalization, and a heightened sensitivity to individual privacy and data security. These trends have been operating for many years, and will continue to shape the evolution of the staffing technologies and processes.

In this chapter we examine some recent trends that are somewhat less pervasive than those mentioned above. But these newer trends have already gained significant ground among some staffing experts, software developers, and workplace psychologists. While these emerging trends may not all expand and define the next generation of staffing processes, they represent the best bets to do so. For each of the areas below, some organizations are already implementing approaches that respond to these trends.

Note that the change drivers behind technology innovation for technology-based staffing that we described in Chapter 1 are relevant for these newer trends also. Specifically, business benefits of efficiency and speed, increased insight and predictive accuracy, and greater strategic impact remain fundamental goals for these HR systems. Newer innovations will need to contribute to these outcomes or they will likely burn out quickly.

Talent Supply-Chain Management

"Talent management" is certainly not a new concept. However, the trend for more integrated HR software systems is a more recent development and will likely continue to have a strong impact on the field of staffing. In short, talent management refers to the processes involved with the acquisition, development, retention, and deployment of people as they move through their tenure in an organization. Much as how supply-chain management works in a production environment, the goal of talent management is to have the right people available at the right time and with the necessary capabilities to meet the needs of the business across time. The staffing processes we have discussed in this book represent a sub-set of talent management concerns. Generally the phrase implies a strategic rather than a purely tactical approach to the issue.[1]

From a technology perspective, the idea that organizations should manage the entire lifecycle of an employee's relationship with their employer raises some new opportunities to contribute strategic value. HR technology systems have evolved to manage single or adjacent functions in the talent management chain (e.g., recruiting and screening tools have usually been separate from performance management tools).

The initial development of technology tools tends to be motivated by the need to improve efficiency at a given point in the talent management process. However, the gains due to efficiency diminish after the initial versions of a software solution are released, and software providers have found that they need to add value in new ways in order to grow their market share. By adding software components together that have not typically been combined into a common system, there is potential to add new insights and strategic value to business operations, and to better align components with business objectives. Conveniently, this approach also allows software providers to move into new market areas by adding more components to create a full talent management "suite" of tools; that is, integrating all aspects of the talent lifecycle managed under one system.[2]

This trend suggests that new combinations of staffing tools with other talent management tools will be assembled. Some examples of how this trend is developing include:

- Integration of the results of screening and testing processes into later phases of the hiring process. For example, the use of test results to shape the interview and on-boarding process around the applicants' specific patterns of strengths and weaknesses.
- A broader range of assessment choices to address an array of skills, abilities, and competencies that are important in changing work environments.
- Use of assessment results to form the basis of performance management and development planning, so that early stages of socialization into an organization can be informed by accurate information about the new employee.
- The use of common frameworks about people (e.g., competency or skill sets) to form the basis of integrated talent management toolsets. These elements can then form the basis for easy communication between systems.
- Integrated tools for conducting analyses of jobs and work that feed the foundational job descriptive information into screening, assessment, performance management, and succession management systems.

Despite the claims of the marking departments of many software companies, no provider has yet created a credible solution for managing all aspects of the talent lifecycle, although many are trying and a few will eventually succeed at some level. New combinations of talent management tools will be attempted and their market acceptance and uptake will depend on the real efficiencies they create and the value of the strategic insights they generate.

Evidence-Based Management

Another accelerating trend is centered on the concept that management practices should be supported by empirical evidence – research that clearly demonstrates the value of one approach over alternatives.[3] The trend has migrated from the healthcare industry, where evidence-based medicine has become a pervasive management philosophy. In some regards, recruitment and staffing technologies are ideally suited to reinforce this trend. Many of the tools and processes we have reviewed in this book grew out of a long history of empirical research within workplace psychology. The requirement to demonstrate the reliability and validity of assessment tools that are used to make decisions about people in the workplace provides a foundation for broader levels of proof of the utility of these approaches. However, if the trend toward requiring evidence for various management practices continues, the implications may extend well beyond assessment validity. Some examples and implications of this trend include:

- Systems will be designed to optimize for the prediction of outcomes that are measured at various stages of the employee lifecycle. For example, HRIS data regarding employee attendance, tenure, and turnover may be used to determine the best sourcing avenues and screening techniques for specific jobs.
- Similarly, job satisfaction and engagement data from culture surveys may be used to calibrate recruitment and selection processes so that the attitudinal fit with a work assignment is considered along with skill fit when designing selection processes.
- Expert systems may assist with complex functions and business rules such as changing passing scores on assessments to adjust for fluctuating job requirements or business conditions.
- Increasing use of tools like prediction markets to determine the viability of new approaches for candidate attraction and recruitment. Prediction markets are large groups of people who provide opinions about new ideas. The technique is most commonly used to estimate the viability and popularity of new product ideas.
- Traditional forms of screening and selection (e.g., resume review, unstructured interviewing) may decline in popularity due to lack of supporting evidence.

Network Organizations and Social Software

Networks are a natural structure for describing human interactions and relationships. A growing bank of research shows that networks have consistent characteristics, whether they are social networks, organizational networks, or even networks of linked web pages.[4] Additionally, organizational operating structures may be viewed as networks, in concert with the typical hierarchical view. Networks are also central to the proliferation of user-created web content – the hallmark of "Web 2.0" approaches to website design that emphasize open, participative, and collaborative online content production.[5] For organizational staffing concerns, social networking software is perhaps the most important example of this development. Social networking sites such as MySpace, Facebook, and LinkedIn provide a rich avenue for the next generation of innovations in organizational recruiting and staffing.

Network-based approaches to understanding organizations and informal groups have multiple implications for staffing practices and technologies:

- Organizations that are explicitly managed as networks may have different kinds of jobs and these may require different skills than jobs in traditional organizations. Therefore the staffing processes that fill these jobs should also adjust. New competencies such as Network Management, Influence across Boundaries, and Using Networks to Drive Change are becoming more common in organizational competency models.
- The popularity of online social networks is changing how recruiters and recruiting tools operate to take advantage of this information. Recruiters are already instructed to look at online profiles of top candidates, but as this trend evolves it is likely that these searches will become more automated and focused. Some networks are designed with an explicit emphasis on professional networking (e.g., LinkedIn), and it is likely that these tools may readily connect to recruiting and staffing sites to enable quick generation of possible leads for applicants. Social network sites also have the advantage of providing recruiters with "passive candidates" – those elusive individuals who may be the perfect candidates for a particular job, but who are already employed and not actively looking for a new job.
- New forms of assessment may also emerge that allow organizations to make better use of the information mined from social networks. These may include externally facing tools that look for keywords in profiles, similar to resume search tools that were popular in the late

1990s, as well as internal tools that allow organizations to identify and map the individuals who are central to the informal networks in their organizations.

Self-Service HR

One of the major benefits of online technologies stems from the fact that the Internet is available anywhere and anytime there is a connection available. This powerful capability is a driver for the growing trend towards self-service staffing processes. As we examined in detail in Chapter 9, there are also some serious drawbacks encountered when using some forms of assessment in an unsupervised Internet-based selection process. How can you tell who is taking the test? How can you protect the security of the assessment content, so that it is not simply passed from user to user? These concerns have motivated research and development into methods for reducing these risks and removing barriers to self-service staffing processes.[6] Examples of these methods include:

- Use of item banking and adaptive testing technologies. Rather than traditional fixed forms, assessments can be constructed from large banks of items such that each candidate receives a unique alternate form of the assessment.[7] Adaptive testing uses advanced theories of assessment construction to create tests that are uniquely calibrated to each test taker. Generally, the approach uses each test-taker response to estimate his or her ability level on the concept being measured. Easier or harder test questions are then chosen to better verify that the estimate is correct. These approaches have several advantages for Internet-delivered testing: fewer test questions need to be asked so the experience is shorter, each test taker only sees a small portion of the available questions, and each test taker gets a unique combination of questions so that the risk of cheating is reduced. This form of testing has been available for decades, but Internet-based versions are now emerging for use in high-volume hiring programs.
- Use of data forensics to detect cheating and security breaches. High-volume users of tests and other assessments are investigating the resulting information for signs of trouble. It is now commonplace for desirable employers to find that secure portions of their

assessment process, complete with example answers, have been posted on blogs or job hunting sites. Advanced data analytics allow organizations to detect unusual patterns of responses that arise when content has been compromised in this manner. Expect these technologies to advance in the coming years.

- Embedded security information. Another emerging approach to the detection of security breach involves presenting unique codes or other identifiers within the assessment content that is viewed by a particular applicant. These technologies allow for the identification of the user who shares content with others in a manner that is inconsistent with their usage agreement. Once identified, organizations can then disqualify candidates who violate content security principles and thereby discourage future security breaches.
- Video and biometric technologies. Web cameras, fingerprint reader mouse devices, and other technologies are beginning to appear in remote assessment programs as a means of supervising and authenticating candidates remotely.

New Technologies to Drive Efficiency, Realism, Interest, and Engagement

Of course, advances in computer and Internet technologies will continue. These innovations will undoubtedly have big implications for automated recruiting and staffing. A few of the more recent innovations that are crossing into the realm of recruiting and staffing are described below.

- Use of animation and avatars in assessment. Simulation-based assessment, in particular, is amenable to the incorporation of game-like interfaces where the user can interact with animated characters that present work-related challenges. Candidates are assessed on their responses and interactions just as they would be in live role-plays and other forms of assessment that use simulated work tasks. These techniques are already in use for some forms of assessment such as post-training evaluations. They offer some of the advantages of human interaction without the cost of trained role-players. However, the jury is still out regarding the advantages they offer for accurate and valid measurement.

- Use of online games and competitions. In an effort to appeal to generations raised on computer games, some recruiting sites are including competitive activities. These can range from activities that provide an engaging way to learn company information by exploring simulated work environments to collaborative work environments that allow future employers to sample the work of potential job seekers.
- Internal (back-end) systems that allow recruiters and hiring managers to assemble information dashboards to monitor and facilitate talent management functions within their span of control. The combination of expert systems, new assessment approaches, and componentized software services may allow for a greater range of functionality to facilitate global hiring processes.

Concluding Thoughts

Regardless of future technology advancements, the fundamental issue for recruiting and staffing processes will remain: making good decisions about people. Automated staffing tools must collect data that are meaningful, processed effectively for the purpose, and available to the right person at the right time to have an impact on decision quality. For organizations, these tools must drive efficiencies, add new insights, or add new levels of value for informing organizational strategy. For individuals, these processes minimally must respect participants' time, privacy and dignity; ideally, they add interest, facilitate self-insight, and generate engagement.

To be sure, there will always be barriers to the use of structured processes for decision-making about people. Many of these stem from the mistaken perception that our own unassisted judgment is better than an objective processes. However, technology can act to reduce these objections by standardizing and simplifying the methods for staffing organizations. Professionals who work in these areas are encouraged to stay informed about the advances that technology can offer these functions. The benefits to those who do are potentially great, as organizational talent moves to the forefront as a key differentiator among business organizations.

Appendix

Assessment Fundamentals

If you are implementing assessments in your organization as part of an installation of an online staffing process, you should ensure the tools are properly developed and validated. The material in this section will help you understand the details and requirements for good assessments.

Criterion-Related Validation

The fundamental concept underlying a criterion-related validation study is the relationship between assessment scores and job performance. This relationship is commonly expressed in numerical form using an index called the *correlation coefficient*, or synonymously in personnel selection applications, the *validity coefficient* (r).[1] Other approaches to quantifying criterion-related validity are available; however, the validity coefficient is widely used, so we highlight the r index.

In personnel selection, r values vary depending upon the effectiveness of the test, as well as other factors, such as the size and composition of the sample of people included in the validation study, and the nature of the performance criterion measure being predicted. There is no minimum r value required for a test to be useful, so long as the reported value is larger than zero and it is based on a large enough sample to be stable. Generally speaking, r values in the range of .20

The Validity Coefficient (*r*)

The *r* index represents the degree of linear association between two measures, such as a test score and a job performance measure. People vary in their scores on tests and in their levels of job performance; *r* reflects the degree of covariation between the two measures. The value of *r* is zero when there is absolutely no association between the two measures; *r* ranges up to +1.0 when there is a perfect positive association (e.g., people are rank ordered the same on test score and job performance), or down to −1.0 when there is a perfect negative association between measures (e.g., people are ranked in the opposite direction on test score vs. job performance). For some criteria, such as job productivity, we want to see a positive *r* with test scores; for other criteria, such as quitting the job, a negative *r* with test scores is desirable. To the extent that the observed *r* value is greater (less) than zero, we have evidence of criterion-related validity for the test. Because each reported *r* is actually an estimate of the *true* relationship, a statistical probability (p) is also reported. By convention, practitioners look for a probability of .05 or less ($p < .05$) that the observed *r* could be a due to an artifact of the sample – a chance occurrence.

to .30 are common for a single test, and higher values may be obtained by combining multiple predictors that are correlated with the criterion, but not with each other (e.g., cognitive ability and personality tests). An instrument with a lower validity coefficient can be quite useful in a selection program with a very low selection rate (e.g., selecting the top 10%), while a test with a high validity coefficient may be rendered virtually useless in a selection program with a very high selection rate (e.g., screening out only 5% of candidates), depending upon the selection rate and the base rate for successful job performance in the workforce. Figures A.1a–1c illustrate different *r* values in a plot of 30 test scores and corresponding performance measures.

Some important considerations for establishing criterion-related validity evidence include:

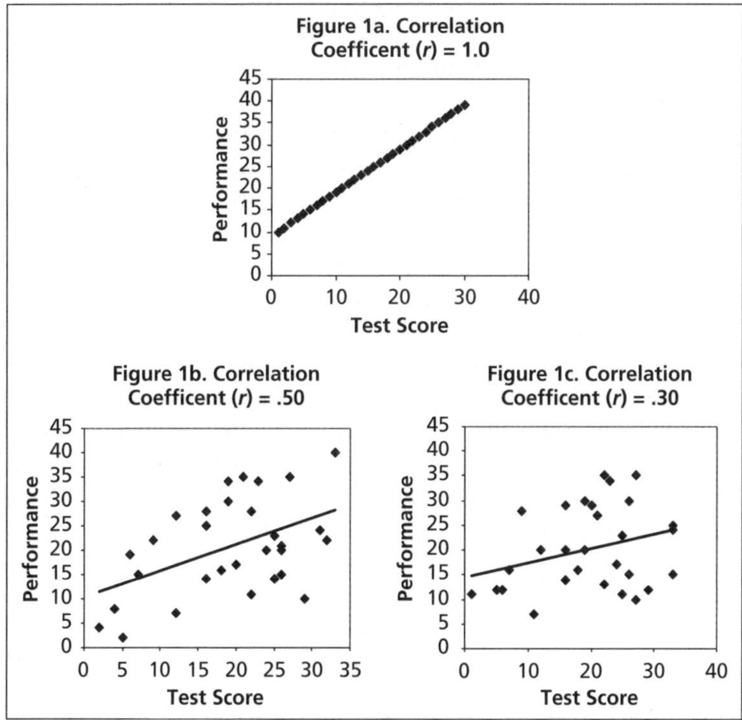

Figure A.1a–1c Correlation coefficient examples illustrating three different test score–job performance relationships

- *Feasibility.* To conduct a successful study, it is necessary to have a sufficient sample of people who are representative of the job, and for whom test and criterion data are available. Generally, the larger the sample the better, until you reach the thousands; conducting a study based on fewer than one hundred subjects runs the risk of failing to detect a significant relationship when one may exist (what statisticians refer to as "low statistical power").
- *Design.* Criterion-related studies may be conducted by testing job applicants, and later gathering job performance measures and

analyzing relationships (known as a predictive design), or by testing job incumbents and gathering job performance data at the same time (known as a concurrent design). Variations on these two approaches are common.

- *Job analysis.* A review of job duties and requirements is an important component of criterion-related validation, both to guide the initial choice of test instruments, and to ensure that the criterion measures reflect important job components.
- *Criteria.* The criterion measures should reflect job-related activities or other outcomes to be predicted. These should be free from bias, and representative of important components of the job.
- *Technical documentation.* A detailed technical report should be written that documents in detail the procedure, test and criterion instruments, research sample, and validity results (e.g., validity coefficients and statistical confidence levels). Professional and legal standards and guidelines are very specific about the requirements for technical documentation of criterion-related validation evidence.

Content Validation

As noted in Chapter 3, content validation provides another approach to justifying the appropriateness of an assessment for a given job. This process uses expert judgment of the relationship between the assessment content and the content of the job (this judgment is often referred to as a "linkage"). Some important considerations for establishing content-based validity evidence include:

- *Feasibility.* To conduct a successful content validation study, it is necessary to have access to well-qualified subject matter experts (SMEs) to participate in the study. Also, the job for which the test is to be validated should be relatively stable with regard to work performed and required knowledge, skills, abilities, and other characteristics (KSAOs).
- *Design.* Key components in the study design include the selection of SMEs, definition of the content area to be assessed, choosing or developing test content, and conducting test review and content linkage sessions. While the emphasis is on content review, it is still

important to gather data to demonstrate that the scores yielded by content-based assessments provide useful measurement for the intended examinee group.

- *Job analysis.* Conducting a thorough and comprehensive review of job duties, behaviors and KSAOs is an important component of content-based validation, to provide a basis for defining content areas to be measured by the test. During this phase, it is also important to establish which KSAO elements are required before hire (and thus are appropriate to assess for selection purposes) vs. learning post-hire in training or on the job.
- *Technical documentation.* A detailed technical report should be written that documents details of the job analysis, content areas, how the job experts were selected, and test-review and test-job-content linkages. Professional and legal standards and guidelines are very specific about the requirements for technical documentation of content-based validation evidence.

Reliability Indices

As we described in Chapter 3, the reliability of an assessment relates to how consistently it measures what it is intended to measure. Various types of errors can be introduced into an assessment and, accordingly, corresponding indices of reliability have been developed to quantify the consistency of measurement instruments with reference to different potential errors.

Reliability can be expressed using the same correlation coefficient (r) described earlier in the discussion of validity. Reliability coefficients are derived by correlating the scores obtained in repeated administrations of an instrument to a group of people under different conditions; for example, across time, across alternate forms, across items, or across assessors (raters). The reliability coefficient is denoted $r_{xx,}$ where the subscript "xx" indicates the correlation of the instrument with itself, reflecting consistency. This is distinguished from the validity coefficient, which is denoted as r_{xy}, where the subscript "xy" denotes the correlation of the instrument score (x) with an external criterion measure (y).

The reliability coefficient r_{xx} can also be expressed in test score units called the standard error of measurement (SEM). The SEM

Table A.1 Reliability methods, errors addressed, common applications, and additional considerations

Reliability Estimation Method	*Types of Errors Addressed*
Test–retest: correlate scores on the same instrument administered to the same group at different times.	• Instability • Administration errors
Equivalence: correlate scores on alternate forms of the same instrument administered at the same time.	• Improper content sampling • Administration errors
Internal consistency: correlate item scores, or random subtest scores, within a single instrument.	• Improper content sampling
Assessor reliability: correlate ratings or scores assigned by different evaluators to the same group of people	• Scoring

provides a convenient way to describe test score precision. To oversimplify, SEM is an estimate of the variation in scores that would be expected if the assessment were taken many times by the same person. A range of ±1 SEM around an observed score represents the range of scores that would be obtained 68% of the time; a range of ±2 SEM represents the range of scores that would be obtained 95% of the time.

Table A.1 outlines four reliability estimation methods, along with types of measurement errors that they address, typical applications, and considerations for their use and interpretation.

Applications	Considerations
• Test measures more than one trait. • Content is *not* easily remembered. • Speeded and time-restricted tests of perceptual skills. • Test results are to be used for a long period of time.	• Practice effects. • Fatigue effects. • Time interval between testing.
• Test measures more than one trait. • Content *is* easily remembered. • Speeded and time-restricted tests • Alternate test forms available.	• Comparability of alternative form scores.
• Only one test administration is possible. • Test measures only one trait. • Test is *not* time-restricted.	• Similarity of content. • Longer tests tend to be more reliable.
• Judgments are made by raters who observe behavior or outcomes and assign scores.	• Using multiple raters increases reliability.

If you would like to know more about methods and considerations for calculating and using reliability and SEM information, we encourage you to refer to an introductory measurement statistics text (several are outlined in the recommended readings for this chapter).

Measurement Scales

Assessment scores may be reported on a variety of different scales of measurement. The examples in the box overleaf represent typical score scales that are used in personnel selection.

Common Test Score Scales In Personnel Assessment

- *Raw scores:* these are the observed, unadjusted scores that result from the attribute measure; they are generally not interpretable, beyond telling you that the candidate attempted and was successful in answering some number of questions.
- *Percentile scores:* defined earlier as *the score below which a certain percentage of people fall*, percentile scores provide a fine-grained description of the examinee's standing on the attribute relative to others. One important consideration for the use of percentiles is whether the instrument supports the ranking of people into 99 distinct categories; often we find that the instrument effectively distinguishes only 10 performance levels or bands, so we might identify 10 groups, called *deciles*, or even 5 groups, call *quintiles* (five bands separated by the 20, 40, 60, and 80th percentiles).
- *Standard scores* (z and T scores): test scores may be transformed and expressed as a function of their proximity to the mean score, relative to a distribution of scores. These are called standard scores. Two common standard scores are z and T: z scores have a mean of 0 and a standard deviation (SD) of 1; T scores are scaled to have a mean of 50 and an SD of 10 (T scores are convenient because they avoid negative scores). Standard scores indicate how far above or below average your candidate scored in SD units. For example when $z = -1.0$, we know the candidate scored 1 SD below the mean.[2] Standard scores can be scaled to any mean and SD that is convenient for the user.
- *Normalized scores:* test scores may be transformed so that the shape of the score distribution changes, as needed, to conform to certain properties of a perfect bell curve. When the distribution is "normal" standard scores can be interpreted with reference to points in the test score distribution (e.g., when $z = 1$, we know that that candidate scored at the 84th percentile).

Fairness in Testing

Another important aspect of the use of selection tests and procedures relates to the *fairness* associated with the use of the scores. In the scientific community, there is no agreement on a single definition of test fairness, although four possible types of fairness have been identified:[3]

- *Equal group outcomes.* Differences in passing rates for subgroups of interest may suggest the procedure be examined for bias; however, most agree that pass rate differences alone do not indicate bias per se.

- *Equitable treatment.* All examinees should have equal access to practice materials, performance feedback, retest opportunities, and other testing conditions.
- *Comparable opportunity to learn.* Subject matter covered in the test should be available to all examinees. This applies primarily to content-based tests, such as job knowledge tests for which training is available.
- *Lack of predictive bias.* The predictions of job performance based on test scores for all examinees combined are adequate to predict job performance for subgroups of interest.

In the United States, federal testing guidelines focus on two areas related to fairness in selection procedures: predictive bias and group outcomes.

The *Uniform Guidelines on Employee Selection Procedures* call for studies of potential unfairness in assessment procedures when technically feasible, defining "unfairness" as follows:

> When members of one race, sex, or ethnic group characteristically obtain lower scores on a selection procedure than members of another group, and the differences in scores are not reflected in differences in a measure of job performance, use of the selection procedure may unfairly deny opportunities to members of the group that obtains the lower scores.[4]

Under this definition, a selection procure is not necessarily unfair if differences in subgroup scores are manifested. Rather, the joint relationship between test scores and job performance is examined to determine whether a procedure is unfair.

Differential Prediction Analysis

In practice, measurement specialists apply a statistical method called differential prediction analysis to examine the potential predictive bias (unfairness) of test instruments. Although beyond the scope of this book, it is worth mentioning this procedure so that you will recognize it as an appropriate form of evidence of fairness when reviewing professionally developed instruments. Essentially, the procedure entails deriving test-criterion prediction equations for all examinees combined, and separately for subgroups of interest. Parameters of the equations (called slope and intercept) are compared, along with errors in the prediction of job performance (comparing actual job performance vs. performance predicted by the test). If the parameters are not found to differ significantly (within statistical probability), then unfairness is not manifested and the test is considered to be fair.

Adverse Impact Analysis

Although the legal community focuses on predictive bias in defining unfairness, it shifts its attention to equality of outcomes in detecting potential discrimination. In determining whether an employee selection practice is discriminatory, the above-referenced *Uniform Guidelines* require an analysis comparing selection rates among demographic subgroups (e.g., gender, race/ethnicity). The so-called "adverse impact analysis" plays a critical role in the evaluation of staffing programs for potential violations of federal fair employment laws (e.g., Title VII of the Civil Rights Act). To be legal in the United States, selection procedures that have an adverse impact must be justified on the grounds of *business necessity*, which generally means that validation evidence should be available. Adverse impact analysis entails comparing selection rates; two methods are used:

- *The four-fifths (80 percent) "rule of thumb."* The selection rate for each subgroup must be at least 80% of the rate for the group with the highest rate. For example, if the job applicant selection rates are 50% male and 40% female, the adverse impact ratio for females is .80 (40/50 = .80), which meets the 80% rule and would not be considered to be first blush evidence of adverse impact, or unfair discrimination. This index is called a rule of thumb because there are exceptions.
- *Statistically significant differences in selection rates.* When large numbers of selections are made, the adverse impact ratio may be subjected to further analysis even when the 80% rule is satisfied. A test of statistical significance of the observed difference in selection rates may be used as evidence of adverse impact. A statistical significance test determines the probability of obtaining the observed result purely by chance (e.g., if selection were random). If the prob-

ability is more than 1 out of 20 (5%), then by convention we would conclude that the observed result is not statistically significant; i.e., there is no adverse impact.

Selected References for Further Reading

Allen, M. J., & Yen, W. M. (2001). *Introduction to measurement theory.* Monterey: Brooks/Cole.

Cascio, W. F. (1991). *Costing human resources: The financial impact of behavior in organizations.* Boston: Kent Publishing.

Cascio, W. F., Alexander, R. A., & Barrett, G. V. (1988) Setting cutoff scores: Legal, psychometric, and professional issues and guidelines. *Personnel Psychology*, 41(1), 1–24.

Guion, R. M., & Highhouse, S. (2006). *Essentials of personnel assessment and selection.* New York: Lawrence Erlbaum Associates.

Guilford, J. P., & Fruchter, B. (1978). *Fundamental statistics in psychology and education.* New York: McGraw-Hill.

Miner, M. G., & Miner, J. B. (1979). *Analysis of Uniform Guidelines on Employee Selection Procedures.* Washington, DC: Bureau of National Affairs, Inc.

Notes

Chapter 1

1 Landefeld, J. S., & Fraumeni, B. M. (2001). Measuring the new economy. *Survey of Current Business, 81* (March), 23–40.

2 Johnson, W. B. (1987). *Workforce 2000: Work and workers for the 21st century*. Washington, DC: Hudson Institute and the U.S. Dept. of Labor.

3 For a broader discussion of the trends and issues associated with the rising importance of human talent in organizations, see Michaels, E., Handfield-Jones, H., & Axelrod, B. (2001). *The war for talent*. Boston: Harvard Business School Press.

4 Friedman, T. L. (2005). *The world is flat: A brief history of the twenty-first century*. New York: Farrar, Straus and Giroux.

5 iLogos. (2003). *Global 500 website recruiting: 2003 survey*. Author.

6 See the following sources for further information on these early trends:

Cappelli, P (2001). Making the most of online recruiting. *Harvard Business Review, 79*, 139–146.

iLogos. (2001). *Trends in Fortune 500 careers website recruiting*. Taleo Research: Author.

National Telecommunications and Information Administration (2002). *A nation online: How Americans are expanding their use of the Internet*. Washington, DC: U.S. Department of Commerce.

Pew Research Center. (2007). Pew Internet and American Life Project. Current trends. www.pewinternet.org/trends.asp. Downloaded June 1, 2008.

Stone, D. L., Lukaszewski, K. M., & Isenhour, L. C. (2005) e-Recruiting: Online strategies for attracting talent. In H. Guental, D. L. Stone, & E. Salas (Eds.), *The brave new world of eHR: Human resources in the digital age* (pp. 54–103). San Francisco: Wiley & Sons.

7 National Telecommunications and Information Administration. (2002). Op. cit.
8 Lev, B. (2001). *Intangibles: Management, measurement, and reporting.* Brookings Institution Press.

Chapter 2

1 Hagel, J., & Brown, J. S. (2001). Your next IT strategy. *Harvard Business Review*, October, 105–113.

Chapter 3

1 Collins, J. (2001). *Good to great.* New York: HarperCollins.
2 Schmidt, F. L., & Hunter, J. E. (1998). The validity and utility of selection methods in personnel psychology: Practical and theoretical implications of 85 years of research findings. *Psychological Bulletin, 124*, 262–274.
3 Cascio, W. (2001). *Costing human resources: The financial impact of behavior in organizations.* Boston: Kent.
4 For example, see the state of Wyoming's website: www.wyomingworkforce.org/resources/turnover.aspx.
5 See: www.bls.gov.
6 American Educational Research Association, American Psychological Association, National Council on Measurement in Education. (1999). *Standards for educational and psychological testing.* Washington, DC: American Educational Research Association.
7 A summary of this research is provided by Frank Schmidt and John Hunter (1998). Op. cit.
8 Meherans, W. A., & Lehman, I. J. (1984). *Measurement and evaluation in education and psychology.* New York: Holt, Rinehart.
9 American Educational Research Association, American Psychological Association, National Council on Measurement in Education. (1999). Op. cit.
10 Society for Industrial and Organizational Psychology. (2003). *Principles for the validation and use of personnel selection procedures*, 4th edn. Bowling Green, OH: Author.
11 International Test Commission. (2005). *International guidelines on computer-based and Internet delivered testing, Version 2005.* Author.
12 Codified as Subchapter VI of Chapter 21 of Title 42 of the United States Code, 42 U.S.C. § 2000e [2].
13 Codified as Chapter 14 of Title 29 of the United States Code, 29 U.S.C. § 621 through 29 U.S.C. § 634.

14 Codified as 42 U.S.C. § 12101.

15 U.S. Equal Employment Opportunity Commission, U.S. Civil Service Commission, U.S. Department of Justice, and U.S. Department of Labor. (1978). *Uniform guidelines on employee selection procedures. Federal Register, 43*(166), 38295–38309.

Chapter 4

1 Hunter, J. E., & Hunter, R. F. (1984). Validity and utility of alternative predictors of job performance. *Psychological Bulletin, 96*, 72–98.

2 For an excellent summary of the various pitfalls affecting human judgment, see Kahnneman, D., & Tversky, J. (1982). *Judgment under uncertainty: Heuristics and biases.* Cambridge: Cambridge University Press.

3 Huffcutt, A. I., & Aurthur, W., Jr. (1994). Hunter and Hunter (1984) revisited: Interview validity for entry-level jobs. *Journal of Applied Psychology, 79*, 184–190.

Chapter 5

1 Premack, S. L., & Wonous, J. P. (1985). A meta-analysis of realistic job preview experiments. *Journal of Applied Psychology, 70*, 706–719.

2 Sinar, E. F., Paquet, S. L., & Reynolds, D. H. (2003). Nothing but 'Net? Corporate image and web-based testing. *International Journal of Selection and Assessment, 11*, 150–157.

3 Levering, R., & Moskowitz, M. (2008). 100 Best companies to work for. *Fortune*, February 4, 2008. Readers are encouraged to review the current list; the companies listed in the text represent large employers across a range of industries that were reported in the 2008 list and had been on the list for multiple years.

4 Cober, R., Brown, D., Levy, P., Keeping, L., & Cober, A. (2003). Organizational web sites: Web site content and style and determinants of organizational attraction. *International Journal of Selection and Assessment, 11*, 158–169.

5 Kristof-Brown, A. L., Zimmerman, R. D., & Johnson, E. C. (2005). Consequences of individuals' fit at work: A meta-analysis of person–job, person–organization, person–group, and person–supervisor fit. *Personnel Psychology, 58*, 281–342. Also see: Boswell, W. R., Boudreau, J. W., & Tichy, J. (2005). The relationship between employee job change and job satisfaction: The honeymoon-hangover effect. *Journal of Applied Psychology, 90*, 882–892.

6 This discussion has been adapted from Reynolds, D. H., & Dickter, D. N. (In Press). Technology and employee selection. In J. L Farr &

N. Tippins (Eds.), *Handbook of Employee Selection*. Psychology Press: New York. See this source for a summary of related research on the issues described here.

7 For example, see Buster, M. A., Roth, P. L., & Bobko, P. (2005). A process for content validation of education and experienced-based minimum qualifications: An approach resulting in federal court approval. *Personnel Psychology*, *58*, 771–799.

8 U.S. Department of Labor. (2005). Obligation to solicit race and gender data for agency enforcement purposes; final rule. *Federal Register*, *70* (194), 58947–58961.

Chapter 6

1 Deductive reasoning is defined as "The ability to apply general rules to specific problems to produce answers that make sense." (O*Net Online, 2008: http://online.onetcenter.org)

2 See Section 7B of the *Uniform Guidelines*; U.S. Equal Employment Opportunity Commission, et al. (1978). Op. cit.

3 Ibid. See Section 3B.

4 In the United States, EEO-1 reports must be submitted annually to the Joint Reporting Committee for the use of the EEOC and OFCCP. The survey must be filed annually by employers with a hundred or more employees, or employers with federal government contracts of $50,000 or more and fifty or more employees. The survey includes data on the size and location of employer establishments, and demographic breakdowns of the workforce. Further information about the EEO-1 Report is available on the agency's website at www.eeoc.gov.

Chapter 7

1 See, for example, Steckerl, S. (2005). *Electronic recruiting 101*. Electronic Recruiting Exchange, www.ere.net.

Chapter 8

1 World Wide Web Consortium, www.w3.org.

2 Pearlson, K. E., & Saunders, C. S. (2006). *Managing and using information systems: A strategic approach*. Hoboken, NJ: John Wiley & Sons.

3 World Wide Web Consortium, www.w3.org/XML.

4 HR-XML Consortium: www.hr-xml.org.

5 IMS Global Learning Consortium, www.imsglobal.org.

Chapter 9

1 Tippins, N. T., Beaty, J., Drasgow, F., Gibson, W. M., Pearlman, K., Segall, D. O., & Shepherd, W. (2006). Unproctored Internet testing in employment settings. *Personnel Psychology*, *59*, 189–225.
2 International Test Commission. (2005). Op. cit.
3 Association of Test Publishers. (2002). *Guidelines for computer-based testing*. Washington, DC: Author.
4 CyberSource. (2008). 9th Annual Fraud Report, http://search.cybersource.com.
5 International Test Commission. (2005). Op. cit.
6 Weiner, J. A., & Morrison, J. (2008). *Unproctored online testing: Environmental conditions and validity.* Paper presented at the 22nd Annual Conference of the Society for Industrial and Organizational Psychology, San Francisco.
7 McCabe, D. L., Treviño, L. K., & Butterfield, K. D. (2001). Cheating in academic institutions: A decade of research. *Ethics and Behavior*, *11*(3), 219–232.
8 Hough, L. M., Eaton, N. K., Dunnette, M. D., Kamp, J. D., & McCloy, R. A. (1990). Criterion-related validities of personality constructs and the effect of response distortion on those validities. *Journal of Applied Psychology*, *75*, 581–595.
9 Weiner, J. A., & Ruch, W. W. (2006). *Effects of cheating in unproctored Internet based testing: A Monte Carlo investigation.* Paper presented at the 21st Annual Conference of the Society for Industrial and Organizational Psychology, Dallas, Texas.
10 U.S. Department Of Commerce, National Telecommunications and Information Administration. (September 2004). *A nation online: Entering the broadband age*. Washington, DC: Author.
11 Pew Research Center. (2007). Op. cit.
12 Reynolds, D. H., & Lin, L. (2003). An unfair platform? Subgroup reactions to Internet selection techniques. In T. N. Bauer (Chair), *Applicant reactions to high-tech recruitment and selection methods.* Symposium conducted at the meeting of the Society for Industrial and Organizational Psychology, Orlando, FL.

Chapter 10

1 U.S. Census Bureau. (2003). *The Hispanic population in the United States: March 2002*. Current Population Report P20-545. Washington, DC: Author.

2 Pew Hispanic Center/Kaiser Family Foundation. (2002). *2002 National survey of Latinos: Summary of findings*. Washington, DC: Author.
3 www.ethnologue.com. Downloaded August 5, 2008.
4 Weiner, J. A. (2006). *Testing ESL candidates in the US: Measurement issues and findings*. Presentation at the 21st Annual SIOP Conference, Dallas, TX.
5 See: www.actfl.org.
6 See: www.atanet.org.
7 Hambleton, R. K., Merenda, P. F., & Spielberger, C. D. (2005). *Adapting educational and psychological tests for cross-cultural assessment*. Hillsdale, NJ: Lawrence Erlbaum.
8 Sireci, S. G. (2005). Using bilinguals to evaluate the comparability of different language versions of a test. In Hambleton et al. (Eds.), *Adapting educational and psychological tests for cross-cultural assessment*. Hillsdale, NJ: Lawrence Erlbaum.
9 See: www.intestcom.org.

Chapter 11

1 This program, and the EU laws to which it relates, is described at www.export.gov/safeharbor.
2 See www.export.gov/safeharbor for an expanded discussion of the privacy principles.
3 FTC v. Toysmart.com, 2000.
4 http://csrc.nist.gov/publications/nistpubs/800-33/sp800-33.pdf. Downloaded March 15, 2008.
5 A useful overview of computer security requirements can be found in the NIST publication: http://csrc.nist.gov/publications/nistpubs/800-12/800-12-html/chapter1.html. Downloaded March 10, 2008.
6 www.privacyrights.org/ar/ChronDataBreaches.htm. Downloaded March 10, 2008.

Chapter 12

1 Cappelli, P. (2008). Talent management for the 21st century. *Harvard Business Review*, March, 74–81.
2 For additional views on this trend, see Bill Kulik's columns in *HR Executive* magazine. For example, Kulik, B. (2008, March). Who first called it "talent management"? HR Executive Online: www.hrexecutive.com/HRE/story.jsp?storyId=79502486. Downloaded May 21, 2008.
3 Pfeffer, J., & Sutton, R. L. (2006). Evidenced-based management. *Harvard Business Review*, January, 63–74.

4 Barabási, A. L. (2003). *Linked: How everything is connected to everything else and what it means for business, science, and everyday life.* New York: Plume.
5 See Benkler, Y. (2006). *The wealth of networks: How social production transforms markets and freedoms.* New Haven, CT: Yale University Press, for an extended discussion on the role and value of online networks.
6 Ployhart, R. E. (2006). Staffing in the 21st century: New challenges and strategic opportunities. *Journal of Management, 32*(6), 868–897.
7 Gibson, W. M., & Weiner, J. A. (1998). Generating random parallel test forms using CTT in a computer-based environment. *Journal of Educational Measurement, 35*(4), 297–310.

Appendix

1 Guilford, J. P., & Fruchter, B. (1978). *Fundamental statistics in psychology and education.* New York: McGraw-Hill.
2 $z = (X - M)/SD$, where X = observed score, M = mean score for the reference group; SD = standard deviation of score for the reference group. $T = (10^{*}z) + 50$.
3 American Educational Research Association, et al. (1999). Op. cit. Society for Industrial and Organizational Psychology. (2003). Op. cit.
4 Equal Employment Opportunity Commission, et al. (1978). Op. cit. Sec 14(8) (a).

Name Index

Note: Page numbers followed by n and a number indicate endnotes

Alexander, R. A. 193
Allen, M. J. 193
Aurthur, W. 197n3
Axelrod, B. 195n3

Barabási, A. L. 201n4
Barrett, G. V. 193
Bauer, T. N. 199n12
Beaty, J. 199n1
Benkler, Y. 201n5
Bobko, P. 198n7
Boswell, W. R. 197n5
Boudreau, J. W. 197n5
Brown, D. 197n4
Brown, J. S. 31, 196n1
Buster, M. A. 198n7
Butterfield, K. D. 199n7

Cappelli, P. 196n7, 200n1
Cascio, W. F. 193, 196n3
Cober, A. 197n4
Cober, R. 197n4
Collins, J. 196n1

Dickter, D. N. 197n6
Drasgow, F. 199n1
Dubey, A. 31
Dunnette, M. D. 199n8

Eaton, N. K. 199n8

Farr, J. L. 197n6
Fraumeni, B. M. 195n1
Friedman, T. L. 7, 195n4
Fruchter, B. 193, 201n1

Gibson, W. M. 3, 199n1, 201n7
Guental, H. 195n6
Guilford, J. P. 193, 201n1
Guion, R. M. 193

Hagel, J. 31, 196n1
Hambleton, R. K. 200n7, 200n8
Handfield-Jones, H. 195n3
Highhouse, S. 193
Hough, L. M. 199n8
Huffcutt, A. I. 197n3

Hunter, J. E. 196n2, 196n7, 197n1, 197n3
Hunter, R. F. 197n1, 197n3

Isenhour, L. C. 195n6

Johnson, E. C. 197n5
Johnson, W. B. 195n2

Kahnneman, D. 197n2
Kamp, J. D. 199n8
Keeping, L. 197n4
Kristof-Brown, A. L. 197n5
Kulik, B. 200n2

Landefeld, J. S. 195n1
Lehman, I. J. 196n8
Lev, B. 195n11
Levering, R. 197n3
Levy, P. 197n4
Lin, L. 199n12
Lukaszewski, K. M. 195n6

McCabe, D. L. 199n7
McCloy, R. A. 199n8
Meherans, W. A. 196n8
Merenda, P. F. 200n7
Michaels, E. 195n3
Miner, J. B. 193
Miner, M. G. 193
Morrison, J. 199n6
Moskowitz, M. 197n3

Paquet, S. L. 197n2
Pearlman, K. 199n1
Pearlson, K. E. 199n2
Pfeffer, J. 200n3
Ployhart, R. E. 201n6
Premack, S. L. 197n1

Reynolds, D. H. 197n2, 197n6, 199n12
Roth, P. L. 198n7
Ruch, W. W. 199n9

Salas, E. 195n9
Saunders, C. S. 199n2
Schmidt, F. L. 196n2, 196n7
Segall, D. O. 199n1
Shepherd, W. 199n1
Sinar, E. F. 197n2
Sireci, S. G. 200n8
Spielberger, C. D. 200n7
Steckerl, S. 199n1
Stone, D. L. 195n6
Sutton, R. L. 200n3

Tichy, J. 197n5
Tippins, N. 197n6, 199n1
Treviño, L. K. 199n7
Tversky, J. 197n2

Weiner, J. A. 199n6, 199n9, 200n4, 201n7
Wonous, J. P. 197n1

Yen, W. M. 193

Zimmerman, R. D. 197n5

Subject Index

Note: Page numbers followed by n and a number indicate endnotes

ability, definition of 92
adverse impact analysis 192–3
Age Discrimination in Employment Act 1967 49
age gap 5
American Council on the Teaching of Foreign Languages (ACTFL) 154
American Educational Research Association 48
American Psychological Association 48
American Translators Association 155
Americans with Disabilities Act 1990 49–50
animation and avatars 181
applicant, internet *see* internet applicant
applicant pools, precisely defined 87
applicant tracking systems (ATSs) 61, 105–16
  archiving 115
  customization v configuration 115–16
  data storage 114
  hiring managers use of 110–11
  HR specialists' use of 111–12
  integrating with HRIS 118
  job requisitions 107–9
  quality assurance and compliance monitoring 111–12
  recruiters' use of 107–10
  reports 114
  security 111, 112
  strategic analytics 112
Application Service Provider (ASP) 28, 121
"Apply Now" step 78–80
assessment
  adaptive testing 180
  biodata 94
  cheating 44, 85, 135, 136, 137, 140–2, 145, 180–1, 199n7, 199n9
  checklist 51
  content sampling 44
  cross-cultural 149–61

assessment (*cont'd*)
  definition of terms 39
  format of 94–5
  item banking 145, 180
  level of 98
  measurement scales 189–90
  potential 93–4
  professional standards 48–9, 136, 158–9, 186, 187
  proficiency 92–3
  purpose of 35, 97
  risks 37–8
  risks of self-service 180–1
  score interpretation 45–8
  simulation-based 58–9, 94, 181
  value of 36–7
assessment tools
  brief for hourly jobs 35
  outcomes of effective use 34
  presentation and delivery 101–2
  purpose of 97–8
  reliability 42–5
  score interpretation 45–8
  security 102–3
  timing of tests 102
  types of 91–8
  validity 38–42, 98–9
audio clips 74
automated staffing technologies, rapid growth of 5(fig)
automated tools
  add value to organizations 13
  making a business case for 3–17

background investigations/checks 8, 61, 106, 117, 118, 125–6, 168
backup systems 122
basic qualifications 56, 57, 58, 76, 83, 84, 85–6, 87, 198n8
basic skills, lack of 6
BBBOnline 170
Best Practices and Realities
  Configuration and Implementation of ATS 116
  HR Systems Architecture and Integration 27
bilingual speakers 149–50, 151–2, 156, 157–8, 200n8
biometrics 137, 172, 181
branding standards, recruiting websites 75
business case, making 3–17

California, privacy laws 170
candidate commitment 63–4
candidate pool 70
  diverse 106, 149, 150
  tension between recruitment and selection 70
  unqualified applicants 142
CareerBuilder.com 108
career portals, access to system from 172
careers web page 55–6
cheating 44, 85, 135, 136, 137, 140–2, 145, 180–1, 199n7, 199n9
Cisco Systems 74
Civil Rights Act 1964, Title VII 49, 192
Civil Rights Act 1991 50
civil rights laws 49–50
Civil Service Commission 50, 197n15
client–server architecture 21
communication, with candidates 79, 89, 109–10
company culture, reflected on website 56, 74
compensatory selection process 64–5
competencies, definition 92
computer hardware, effect on assessment 139

computer technology, assessment format and 94–5
configuration v customization 29, 115–16
correlation coefficient see validity coefficient
cost–benefit analysis, integrated staffing system 128–9
cost savings, outsourced services 7
cross-cultural deployment 149–61
customization v configuration 29, 115–16
cut scores 47–8, 141
  definition of 39

data
  archiving 115
  forensics 180–1
  integration 21, 22–5, 106–7, 112–14, 126–8
  integrity 165, 169, 170, 173
  security and privacy 78, 122, 140, 163–74
  storage 114
  tracking systems 105–6
databases
  candidate search 109
  of open positions 56
  resume 71, 80–1, 86
  searching 173
  use during on-boarding 61
Dell 22–3, 25
demographic diversity, assessments 100
demographic subgroups
  access to internet 10
  adverse impact analysis 192
demographic trends, changing 6
desktop computers (PCs) 20–1
diagnostic tool, automated software 102
differential prediction analysis 191–2
digital divide 10, 142
discrimination 49–50, 69, 192
diversity, in workforce 6, 10

e-mails, candidate communication 109–10
employee record 22, 105, 126
employees, add value to organizations 15
employer liability, applicant records and 87
employer overview, recruiting website 73–5
employment branding 15, 55–6, 72, 73–4, 75
encryption 173–4
Enterprise Resource Planning (ERP) 24
environmental conditions, online assessment systems 133–4, 138 , 145, 199n6
Equal Employment Opportunity Commission (EEOC) 49, 50, 197n15, 198n11, 201n4
Ernst & Young 74
errors, measurement 43–4, 188
European Union, data protection 164–5, 171
  Directive on Data Protection 164, 167
evidence-based management 177–8
Extensible Markup Language (XML) 25, 27, 31, 121, 126–8, 198n3, 198n4
  definition of 124

Facebook 179
fair employment law 37, 48, 49–50, 104, 192

fairness, assessment tests 48, 58, 64, 84, 111, 190–3
feedback, online assessment tests 144
fingerprint readers 172, 181
firewalls 27–8, 120
  definition 124
fonts 101
Fortune 100 best companies to work for 73–4, 197n3
fraud, online 137, 141–2, 200n4

games and competitions 182
Gap Inc. 174
General Electric 7
globalization 7, 149–52, 175
Good to Know Boxes
  Making Your Business Case 17
  Questions to Ask Software Providers 31
  Seven Principles of Privacy Protection 165
  Software and Internet Terms 124
  Standards and Guidelines for Test Administration Conditions 136
  Terminology 92
government rules and regulations 16, 69, 85, 99–100, 106, 109, 164, 191
  see also European Union, data protection
Guidelines for Computer-based Testing 136, 200n3

hiring decision, use of databases 60–1
hiring managers
  ATS information for 110–11
  information dashboards for 182
  interview format 59–60
hosted systems 28, 75, 120–1, 124
HR specialists, ATS information for 111–12
HR technology tools, brief history of 4–13
HR XML Consortium 127–8, 198n4
human capital, value to organization 15–16
Human Resource Information Systems (HRIS) 24–5, 105, 113, 126, 178
Hypertext Transfer Protocol (HTTP), definition 124

IMS Global Learning Consortium 128, 198n5
insight and predictive accuracy
  designing systems 62–3
  hiring process 14–15
  newer trends 175–6
instability 44
integration
  processes and information 122–30
  software 22–7
  standards 127–9
  system-to-system messaging 123–5
  web services 26, 123, 124, 125–6
intellectual property, value to organization 15, 140
International Guidelines on Computer-Based and Internet Delivered Testing 49, 136, 196n11
International Test Commission 49, 196n11, 199n2, 199n5
internet
  access of minority groups 10, 142–3

digital divide 10, 142
effect on software design 22
growth of online recruitment 9–11
rapid growth of 4–5, 9–12
web services 26, 123, 124, 125–6
internet applicant, definition of 87
internet applicant rule (2005) 50, 173, 198n8
internet connectivity, effect on assessment 101, 139
interoperability 123–8
interviewing 59–60
ITC Guidelines on Adapting Tests 158, 159

job families 56
job information, recruiting websites 75–6
job knowledge, definition of 92
job seekers
broad pool of 70–1
notice to regarding personal information 166
online steps to follow 54–61
password security 102–3, 172
scarcity of qualified 63
usability of website and 74–5, 76
when becomes applicant 86–7

keyword search tools 81
KSAOs 91–4, 101, 103, 152, 155, 186, 187

labor market 5–6, 65–6, 149–52
language, software 25, 126–8
languages, spoken 149–60
proficiency 153–4
requirements for job 152–3
translating assessments 155–8
legal challenges
cut score results 47
testing program 99–100
legal liability, privacy and security 171
LinkedIn 179
litigation, assessment risks 37–8

mainframe computers 20–1
Marriott 74
measurement scales 189–90
medical screening 61
monitoring, online assessment tests 100, 138, 144
Monster.com 71, 108
multilingual assessment programs 149
multiple-choice questions 94
multiple hurdle selection process 64, 65
MySpace 179

National Council on Measurement In Education 48, 196n6, 196n9
native speakers 151, 156
navigation, online assessments 101–2, 139
networks 178–80, 201n5

Office of Federal Contract Compliance Programs (OFCCP) 50, 85, 86, 87, 173, 198n8, 198n13
online recruiting system, case summary 55
organizational needs and goals, assessment and 36
outsourcing, of HR services 7–8, 136

parsing tools 81, 82
passwords 102–3, 172

performance potential 40
personal characteristic 71, 93–4
  definition of 92
personal information 56–7, 79
  access to 168–9
  complaints and compliance 169–70
  data integrity 169
  definition 167
  European Union and 164–5, 171
  notice to job seekers 166
  security of 140, 163–4
  transfer to third party 167–8
  used for new purposes 167
  see also data security and privacy
Pew Internet and American Life Project 9, 142, 199n11
prediction markets 178
predictive bias 191–2
Principles for the validation and use of personnel selection procedures 49, 136, 158, 159, 196n10
privacy 163–74, 200n2, 200n6
  limited legislation in US 165
professional standards and principles 48–9, 158
profile matching 73, 76–8
protected groups 47, 48, 111, 142
psychological measurement 34–5, 93
psychometrics 34–5, 58, 100

qualifications, basic 56, 57, 58, 76, 84, 85–6, 87, 88, 142, 146, 198n8
questions, online screening 57–8, 82–4

record keeping 50, 86–7, 106, 115
recruiters
  ATS information for 107–10
  information dashboards for 182
recruitment, electronic tools to support 70–1
reference checks 61, 85
reliability, assessment tests 42–5
reliability coefficients 44–5, 187–9
resumes 70–1, 80–2, 88, 93
  databases of 71
return on investment (ROI), assessment programs 36
risks, assessment 37–8, 180–1
role-based security 172–3

Safe Harbor Privacy Principles 165, 167, 168, 170
science-based selection methods 12–13
scores
  cross-cultural equivalence in measurement 157–8
  distribution 46–7
  see also cut scores; test scores
screening 57–8, 80–9
  definition 71
  detail required 87–8
  questionnaire-based 82–3
  resume-centric 80–2
  risks with online 83–5
Secure Socket Layer (SSL) 103, 173
security 102–3, 163–74
  embedded information 181
  encryption 173–4
  history and log files 173
  online assessment 140
  passwords 102–3, 172
  role-based 172–3
security audit 174
selection processes 70, 71–2
  compensatory 64–5
  moving candidates through process 88–9
  multiple hurdle 64, 65
self-service HR, risks of 136, 180–1

sensitive information, definition of 167
service-oriented architecture (SOA) 25–6, 126
Simon & Schuster 7
Simple Object Access Protocol (SOAP) 25, 123
  definition 123
simulation-based assessment 58–9, 94, 181
skill, definition 92
skill level, increasing 5–6
social networking 179
Society for Industrial and Organizational Psychology 49, 196n10, 199n6, 199n9, 199n12, 201n3
software
  access to systems 27–8
  customization v configuration 29, 115–16
  for PCs 21
  maintenance 29–30
Software as a Service (SaaS) 28
software companies 23–4
  questions to ask 31
speed-to-hire 63
spreadsheets, track applicants with 21
staffing system, assembling 62–4
standard error of measurement (SEM) 187–9
standards and guidelines
  content-based validation evidence 187
  criterion-related validation evidence 186
  test administration 136, 158–9
Standards for educational and psychological testing 48–9, 136, 158, 159, 196n6
standardized assessment instruments 33–5
  legal requirements 35
Starbucks 74
state laws, assessment instruments and 50
structured interviews 60, 94–5
system design 117–30
  cost–benefit analysis 128–9
  impact on business processes 129
  IT specialists 129
  growth and change 129
system-to-system messaging 123–5

talent management 176–7
technical support 121–2
technology
  cross-cultural assessment tools 159–60
  online assessment 100–3, 139–44
telephone screening 26
terms and conditions, job application 78–9
test scores 45–8, 183–90
  cut scores 47
  norm-referenced 45–6
  measurement scales 189–90
testing 58
  access to technology 142–3
  candidate perceptions of 143–4
  cheating 44, 85, 135, 136, 137, 140–2, 145, 180–1, 199n7, 199n9
  effect of environmental conditions on 138
  proctored v unproctored 136–8
  security issues 140
  technology issues 139–40

testing (*cont'd*)
  unqualified applicants 142
  see also assessment; assessment tools
third party providers/vendors 7, 56, 75, 76, 113, 120–1
Title VII, Civil Rights Act 1964 49, 192
Toysmart 170
tracking tools 61, 105–16
translation, cross-cultural assessments 155–8
TRUSTe 170
turnover, cost of employee 36–7

Uniform guidelines on employee selection procedures (1978) 50, 99, 191, 192, 197n15
Uniform Resource Locator (URL) 124
unproctored Internet-based testing (UIT) 136–8, 139, 199n1, 199n6, 199n9
  cheating and 141
unqualified applicants 142, 146
user support, cross-cultural 160

validation, assessment tools/instruments 98–9
  content 39–40, 186–7
  criterion-related 40–1, 183–6
  validity generalization 41
validity coefficient (r) 183–6
venture capital funding 17
video clips 74

"war for talent" 6, 195n3
web browser 22, 28, 121
  effect on assessment 139
web cameras 181
web services 26, 123, 124, 125–6
websites
  care with special features 74–5
  designing 69–90
  HR front-office to job seekers 70–1
  privacy and security 163–74
  recruiting site components 72–80
  screening tools 80–6
Wegmans Food Markets 74
workforce, diversity in 6, 10
workplace psychologists, consulting with 100
World Wide Web Consortium (W3C) 123, 199n1, 198n3

XML *see* Extensible Markup Language